THE ULTIMATE FIRST-TIME DAD'S PLAYBOOK

CRACKING THE CODE OF PREGNANCY, MASTERING BABY'S FIRST YEAR, AND PROVEN TIPS FOR NEW DADS

ULTIMATE DADS

TABLE OF CONTENTS

FREE GIFT

Thank you for purchasing our book. We know this time can be hectic, maybe a little overwhelming, so we wanted to give you a head start with the ultimate cheat sheet. From 'Sleep Secrets' (because who doesn't want more sleep?) to 'Feeding Fundamentals' (your crash course in not starving the tiny human) and some super-smooth 'Soothing Hacks'. We haven't forgotten about your partner either, because understanding their needs? Trust me, it's like finding the cheat code to the next level. And, of course, there's a rundown of 'Baby Essentials' and 'Essential Gear'—because gearing up is half the fun, right? Dive in and prep for an amazing journey!

PRAISE FOR ULTIMATE DADS

"Man adopts a role called being a Father so that his child will have something mythical and infinitely important: a protector who will keep a lid on all the chaotic and catastrophic possibilities of life."

— JOHN GREEN

INTRODUCTION: WELCOME TO THE GUILD OF FATHERHOOD

Hey there, new dads! Let's talk about fatherhood, that magical time in a man's life when sleep becomes a distant memory, and your heart grows three sizes bigger. Or so they tell me; I've been too busy changing diapers to notice.

The birth of a new life? It's incredible, and if you're anything like me, you'll be filled with joy, hope, and a healthy dose of fear. Hold your new baby, and you'll realize that nothing else matters. It's a feeling that's as real as that diaper smell. Terrified? Absolutely, but you'll also be thrilled beyond words.

Let's talk about diapers. You're going to face something indescribable. You think you know what to expect? You don't. It's a mess, its chaos, and it stinks. You might laugh, or maybe that's a cry of terror—hard to tell. But trust me; you'll find joy in even the messiest of places.

Balance work and life? You will try. At times you will feel like you've mastered it, and there will be times when you think you are failing at everything. But you'll learn to adjust. You'll find a routine that suits you. That suits your partner. Most importantly it suits your new boss - your baby.

Being a new dad is tough. It's confusing. Sometimes it's just plain odd. You'll be awake during odd hours of the night. You'll be surprised by the amusing faces you can make. You'll experience love in a way you've never before. What about your relationships? They'll evolve. They'll expand. In some cases, they may take surprising detours. That's part of what makes this journey thrilling.

I'm so glad you picked up this book. Dive into the amazing adventure known as fatherhood. This journey isn't about being flawless. It's about showing up. It's about learning from each other. It's about embracing those sleepless nights. Changing those dirty diapers comes with the territory, as does cherishing every adorable giggle.

Guys prepare to put on your hats. It's going to be a wild ride. I promise you it's worth every moment. Get ready to join the dad club!

THE CALM BEFORE THE STORM— PREGNANCY

I n this first chapter, we're not just talking about forming bonds; we're about creating a lifelong, no-returns-accepted connection with this tiny human who's about to turn your world upside down. Don't just sit back—dive in and be part of the journey. After all, nobody ever built a treehouse by watching from the window.

SECTION 1: THE PREGNANCY JOURNEY

I've broken this into the trimesters to get you used to thinking in these terms.

Month 1-3: We're laying the foundation here, folks. Think of it as pouring concrete for the skyscraper of parenthood. Except this one's flesh and blood, and there's no step-by-step manual. Hormones are having a house party and emotions? They're dancing on the tables. It's an exhilarating and slightly terrifying time, kind of like watching a reality TV show where you're the star, hmm, no, your partner is the star, but you are up there as well.

Month 4-6: Now we're into the actual building stage, and boy, does it get real. You'll start to see physical changes. Your partner might be showing a bit, and you'll feel like you're in a science fiction film where everything's familiar and utterly alien. And here's where you can flex those supportive muscles, making her feel like the Wonder Woman she is.

Month 7-9: Welcome to the final stretch! It's like you're on the last lap of a marathon, except you're carrying a watermelon. Your partner, that heroic figure, is dealing with the whole discomfort thing on an epic level. This is your chance to be the superhero's superhero. Massages, sweet surprises, and building that darn crib without cursing too much—it's all part of your training montage.

Here's your month-by-month guide for what's happening in the construction zone:

Month #	Weeks	Activity	Size
1	1-4	Amniotic sac forms; face & eyes develop; heart starts to beat	Slightly smaller than a grain of rice
2	5-9	Limbs, organs, and bone development; heartbeat detectable	About the length of a paperclip
3	10-14	Limbs & extremities formed; all organs present	A weighty 4-inch action figure
4	15-19	Hair & nails grow; can stretch, yawn, make cute faces	A 6-inch sub sandwich minus the extras

Month #	Weeks	Activity	Size
Around this time, your baby can start to hear sounds. It's not just about cute kicks and movement; this is about their brain's ability to recognize and remember the sounds and voices they hear often. Your voice, your partner's laughter, a favorite song — these become familiar to them.			
5	20-24	Baby moves; lanugo & vernix cover the skin	Anywhere between a handy pocket flashlight & a small water bottle
Research shows that your baby can recognize and react to both voices and music, showing preferences for certain rhythms and melodies.			
6	25-30	Translucent skin; eyes open; reacts to sounds; hiccups	About the size of a standard ruler
7	26-29	Fat stores; hearing fully developed; reacts to light	Length of a legal pad, weight of a small bag of flour
Your baby's brain is forming connections, absorbing information that will help them once they're born. Speaking to them, reading stories, and even playing gentle music can foster this connection.			
8	30-34	Rapid brain development; sees & kicks; lungs maturing	Roughly the length of a magazine
9	35-40+	Lungs mature; reflexes coordinated; ready for birth	As long as a rolling pin, weighing in like a decently sized pineapple

And then there's the infamous morning sickness—it's not just a morning thing, and it's as erratic as it sounds. Certain smells or foods trigger nausea and vomiting, and they can hit at any time of the day (Bellefonds, 2022).

I had a buddy who lived through it. Here is his story:

When my girl got hit with the morning sickness wave, everything from melting butter to her once-beloved coffee became her worst enemies. And it wasn't just in the morning! But I had her back. I discovered that ginger snaps or tea could be her best friend during those nauseous moments. It was not magic, but it gave her a bit of relief. I also introduced her to peppermint tea, a fresh, soothing alternative. But there were days when all the tea in China wouldn't cut it. Those times, I would pull out a surprise—a handful of plain Cheerios. This humble snack somehow brought relief. It became our thing—a ritual that brought a smile back to her face. Those tiny hoops became our secret weapon against her nausea battles.

And then comes the main event, where every moment, every doubt, and every crazy food run culminates in something magical: meeting the newest member of your team. No spoiler here, but it will be your life's biggest premiere.

By the way, don't freak out if you start feeling symptoms like backaches or weight gain; it's a known phenomenon called Couvade Syndrome (Pampers, 2022). It's kind of like a sympathy tour minus the merchandise. Weird, right?

Your Role as a Supportive Partner

Supporting your partner might sound like an epic quest, but the little things matter. Here's a level-by-level guide to being the hero she needs:

- **Support Level 1**: Preparing meals, attending doctor's appointments, or a simple back rub. Think of it as the early levels where you learn the controls. And no, pickles and ice cream sandwiches don't count as a balanced meal (or do they?).
- **Understanding Level 2**: Learn the game mechanics— mood swings, cravings, and prenatal care. Knowledge is your power-up.
- **Connection Level 3**: Time to level up that bonding. Talk to the baby, play those lullabies, and prepare for the boss level - birth!

Go ahead read up, learn, and embrace the crazy, beautiful chaos of pregnancy. Build the treehouse with her instead of watching from the window. Get involved, talk to other dads, and prepare for this unpredictable adventure.

Dispelling Common Myths About Pregnancy

My favorite myth is "Dads can't bond with the baby until they're born." Wrong! Your voice can become the soundtrack of their dreams from 18 weeks on.

Around 18 weeks, your soon-to-be-munchkin starts hearing in the womb. Imagine that. They're listening to every word you say, judging your singing skills, and maybe even giving thumbs up or down to your choice of bedtime stories.

Every "well-crafted" sentence you utter becomes their first concert. No pressure, right? You might not be Ed Sheeran, but to your little one, you're a rockstar.

And let's talk brain development here because, in all seriousness, your baby is pulling off some mind-bending stunts. Research shows that they start recognizing the rhythm of your voice (Unicef, n.d.). They're developing the ability to remember sounds and voices they've heard repeatedly during pregnancy. That's right; they've got VIP access to your lullabies.

My second favorite myth has to do with the horizontal tango. Yeah, that doesn't have to stop, either. Just check with the doc, and don't let myths hold you back.

The third myth is that you don't have a lot to do in the construction phase, not true. You are a part of crafting this human being; you're part of creating memories, bonds, and a lifelong connection. And if you're worried about hitting all the right notes, just remember that you're already a superstar to your baby, even if they're already eavesdropping and judging your taste in music.

Embrace every day as they are filled with real, tangible experiences. It's about physical growth, brain development, and emotional connections. The journey might seem overwhelming, but it's woven from everyday moments and simple acts of love and understanding.

Your role as a partner is not about grand heroics but about being present, engaged, and supportive. From understanding the development stages to participating in daily routines, your connection to your partner and your baby grows. This is not a distant, abstract process but a shared experience, rich in details that resonate with everyday life.

SECTION 2: BONDING WITH BABY BUMP

Imagine my wife, and I cozied up on the sofa during those long months of pregnancy. My hand is on her belly, and I'm talking to our future kiddo, sharing life's essential wisdom, like how to find the best cartoons on Saturday mornings.

No secret missions here, just bonding with the little one while they're still in the womb. It isn't just special; it's like a sneak peek of all those bedtime stories to come. It's a real connection and not complicated; it's just love. Lean in and talk; share your thoughts, feelings, or commentary on last night's game. Maybe your future child will agree that the ref made a lousy call!

Those kicks and jabs? That's your baby's way of joining the conversation. No secret codes, just a simple and beautiful way to say, "Hi, Dad!"

The real superstar: Mom, you know, the one making all this happen, your partner, keep her comfortable and happy because when Mom's content, so is the baby (Health Partners, 2021).

Get ready, because being there for your partner means more than holding hands. You're suddenly the in-house chef, chauffeur, supporter, and don't forget the go-to guy for midnight cravings. Run out of orange juice, and you might find yourself in the doghouse.

Tips for Talking, Reading, and Singing to Your Unborn Child

Parenting can be bewildering, especially when connecting with a baby that's not yet here. But it's simpler than you think. Let's break it down:

- **Talking:** Find a quiet moment, touch Mom's belly, and chat. Share your thoughts about the day, your hopes for the future, or anything else. Your baby may not understand the words, but they respond to the warmth and love in your voice. Think of it as an early start on those bedtime stories.
- **Reading:** Dellecese (2015, para. 1) noted that reading to an unborn baby has real benefits. It's a simple way to share your passion for stories or spend quality time with your baby. Pick a favorite childhood book, and don't be shy about making funny voices for the characters. It's all about creating an enjoyable

experience for you and your baby. Your partner might get into it as well.

- **Singing:** Singing to your baby is another wonderful way to bond, even if you're not a natural performer. Whether it's a lullaby, a pop song, or even a jingle from a commercial, your voice can become a comforting sound to your child. You don't have to be pitch-perfect; the joy and love in your voice matters most.

What's most important in these early stages of fatherhood is not your talking, reading, or singing proficiency. It's about being there and being genuine. Share your excitement, your dreams, your love. Make mistakes and laugh at yourself. It's all part of building a connection with your future best friend. For a lot of people this seems downright weird, but there is science to back it up – look it up.

There's no exam to pass, no performance to ace. You and your future child get to know each other in these ways. It's a heart-to-heart connection that begins now and lasts a lifetime. Just take a deep breath and enjoy the journey. You've got this, Dad!

The Long Wait—Story Time

Here is a story Brad shared with us.

My wife had been eagerly waiting to feel our child's kick throughout her pregnancy. I found myself intrigued by her nighttime routine, whispering to the bump, eager to establish a connection. By week 11, our baby started whispering back. She's telling me about these flutters and mini-bounces, and I'm thinking, "Is she just ordering too much takeout?" But nope, it was our kiddo's premiere on the communication scene.

Then came winter. Week 20, specifically, when your toes go numb, and you question why you live where the air hurts your face. So, one frosty eve, as I'm drooling into my pillow, our baby decides to throw a dance party. I'm obviously oblivious to the tiny miracle unfolding. But inside, there's a flurry of life, and my wife is enjoying the front row seat.

Fast forward to the 21st week, my wife felt unwell one night. And as we're sharing that "Oh man, what did we get ourselves into?" look, a gentle nudge comes from below. The missus grins, "Our kiddos chiming in." Placing my hands on her belly, I felt it – a series of jabs and pokes. That night? It wasn't just about the kicks. It was a memory, a beginning, an unspoken pact between us three.

SECTION 3: PREPPING THE NEST

Let's get serious for a moment before we dive into the fun stuff. According to Moon (2019), over 3,500 tiny tots sadly leave us in their sleep due to avoidable accidents like suffocation or strangulation. Heartbreaking, right? We will ensure you have all the information you need to keep that from happening. First on the agenda: the crib. It's like the penthouse suite for your baby, here's a quick crib checklist, for the most essential piece of baby real estate.

Category	Guide to Cozy Cribs
Drop-Side Rail?	Nope, banned. Like mullets. Don't even think about it.
Slat Distance	Keep 'em under 2-3/8 inches. Safety first, fun later.
Firm Mattress	Test it like you'd test a comfy couch. It's gotta bounce back.
Snug Mattress	It should fit like your favorite pair of jeans. And, oh, remove that plastic!
Corner Posts	Either flush or over 16 inches. In between? Not on my watch.
Used Cribs	Older than 10 years? Pass. Check it like a pre-flight checklist.
Safety Notes	Baby on back; keep it bare; no toys; remove mobiles at 5 months; no windows or hanging objects; flame retardant everything.
And Remember...	You've got this. I mean, probably. I'm not a crib expert; I just play one on the internet.

Now, back to our regularly scheduled programming: creating a safe and loving environment for your baby.

We're talking about building the dream pad for your little one. While I'm no Martha Stewart or Bob the Builder, I can at least guide you with the wisdom I've stolen from experts and personal disasters.

First up, grab your partner, choose the room in your home, and make it the coziest, most welcoming place on earth for your baby. Build it together, decorate it, and let it reflect your love for your new family member. Feel the energy, sense the flow, and maybe even summon your inner feng shui wizard. The goal? A baby mansion that's like a mini version of your love and style.

Here is a Pro Tip from Darnell: Lighting can make or break a room. Opt for soft, ambient lighting, especially around the crib. It's a game-changer for those late-night feedings when you don't want to be blinded by overhead lights but need enough illumination for mission 'Diaper Change.'

Now, roll up those sleeves. It's furniture assembly time. Pick up those tools, laugh in the face of those confusing assembly instructions, and remember, building a crib is like assembling IKEA furniture - frustrating, a bit mystifying, but weirdly satisfying when done. Time for the cherry on top: painting and decorating. Unleash the creativity you share, whether you're going for a whimsical wonderland or a serene garden. Working together on this artistic quest, you'll create a world where your little one's dreams can flourish.

This room's not just where dreams happen; it's where dreams start. Make it a masterpiece. Because when your little one takes that first look around, they'll know they've got the best tour guides in the galaxy.

Choosing the Right Baby Gear

Here's what you'll need:

- **Clothing**: Soft, comfy, and practical. Easy to put on and take off, especially during those middle-of-the-night changes.
- **Diapers**: Diapers: Stock up like it's a Black Friday sale. Trust me, you'll need them. Oh, and wipes, creams, and a changing pad. Basically, all the things.
- **Stroller**: Test them out in the store. You will use it often, therefore make sure it fits your lifestyle.
- **Crib**: Safety first here, folks. Look for a sturdy crib with adjustable mattress height and a snug-fitting mattress.
- **Highchair**: You'll need this later, but look for one that is easy to clean because messes will happen.

- **Baby Carrier**: Handy for when you need to take your baby and have your hands free. It's your way of keeping the little one close while having your hands free to grab a much-needed coffee. Find one that fits you comfortably.

Matt wanted to chime in with this Pro Tip: Watch for multi-use baby gear. A few highchairs can transform into toddler seats, and certain cribs can convert into toddler beds. Think of it as unlocking a bonus level in your parenting game.

The Importance of Baby-Proofing and How to Do It Right

Usually, it is recommended to baby-proof your house before the baby starts crawling; however, it would be a no-brainer for you to acquire a bit of knowledge before the baby's arrival. Doing it early? That's like preparing for the villain before they even hatch their evil plan.

Many things can go wrong when a baby is in the mix. You should remember that everything is dangerous to the baby, from the electric sockets and stairs to the furniture, doors, windows, and floors. However, your curious and fearless baby sees this lair as the ultimate playground, ready to explore and conquer every nook and cranny.

You know how you can leave your stuff lying around, and it's okay? That's about to change. Babies are curious creatures, and they'll explore every inch of your home.

Here's your battle plan:

- Crawl around and see what might attract those little hands. You'll be surprised what you find at baby-eye-level.
- Lock up those cabinets and drawers, especially the ones with things you don't want in a baby's mouth.
- Cover those electrical outlets. They're fascinating to little fingers.
- Safety gates must be at the top and bottom if you have stairs.
- Tie up or hide cords, anchor heavy furniture to the wall, and cushion sharp furniture edges.
- Regularly check toys for loose parts or sharp edges. And use non-slip mats to keep those little feet stable.

Remember, babyproofing isn't about putting your little adventurer in a bubble. It's about giving them the world on safer terms because every superhero starts with a secure home base.

There you have it, level 3 complete! You've prepped the nest and are now ready for the ultimate adventure. Keep those extra lives handy because the next level is all about surviving those sleepless nights. Game on!

FATHERHOOD QUEST - THE DAD ODYSSEY

Welcome to your first "Fatherhood Quest," arguably the most epic journey since Frodo's trek to Mordor. And by "epic," I mean more diapers and fewer dragons. We've covered heaps, now don your "New Dad" armor and charge into the fray. If anyone can make babyproofing look like an Olympic sport, it's... probably not us, but darn it, we're giving it our best shot!

Level 1: Chatting With the Bump

Alright, future world's-best-dad, your quest begins here. Get familiar with that growing baby bump. And by "familiar," I'm talking heart-to-heart chats, decoding baby Morse code via kicks. (Heads up: a triple kick isn't the baby's secret message for "More ice cream, please."). Bend down, share tales of your day, sing that song stuck in your head, or recite stats from last night's game. Think of this as your pre-baby bonding sesh.

Level 2: Building the Baby Palace

Welcome to "Extreme Makeover: Babyproof Edition." Gone are the days when your living room resembled a frat house post-party. It's time to transform that space into a miniature monarch's domain. Notice those pointy coffee table edges? Yep, it's time for cushion action. And those enticingly open drawers? Whack on child locks; to those tiny fingers, it's a treasure waiting to be discovered. Your mission, should you choose to accept it, is to prep your space for the baby without turning it into a rubber room.

Level 3: Gear Up and Roll Out

Have you ever attempted to conquer a mall on Black Friday? Now, imagine doing it with a checklist of baby must-haves. Picture 'Mission Impossible,' but instead of sneaking through laser alarms, you're deciphering the enigma of stroller choices on a budget. And a quick pro tip about onesies: they don't come in grown-up sizes (don't ask how I know). Dive headfirst into the realm of baby gear shopping. Patience isn't just a virtue; it's a secret weapon.

As you check off these challenges, envision the sweet sound of "level up" game chimes. The twist? Each achievement unlocks more dad duties. Ah, the wonders of parenthood. Your partner, the ever-growing bump, and your soon-to-be perpetually tired self are all relying on you. Grasp that tepid coffee, seize the day, and here's a reality check: if I can stumble through fatherhood with more laughs than tears, you've got this, too. Let's make "Dad Mode" the new definition of cool (or, at the very least, side-splittingly funny).

2

THE GRAND ARRIVAL—BIRTH

Welcome to the ultimate boss level in the video game of life. In this chapter, we'll spotlight your role during childbirth. We emphasize the importance of preparation, presence, and understanding to enhance the birth experience for both parents. Dive into the intensity and magic of the delivery room, that transformative space where you evolve into a dad. We aim for a raw and honest perspective on birth's emotional and physical aspects, empowering you to actively participate and support your partner. Get ready to hit the "Start" button on your parenting journey!

SECTION 1: BIRTH PLANS AND BAG PACKS

Alright, Player One, here's your strategy guide for the high-stakes game of childbirth. Two main plays: vaginal birth and C-section. Think of vaginal birth like reaching the end zone in a classic game—it's common and often labeled as "natural." But games can throw curveballs, and sometimes complications require a switch to the C-section play. Always consult with your health professional before locking in your game plan.

To be truly prepared, you've got to understand various birth scenarios and have answers to these three game-changers, as pointed out by Ben-Joseph (2018):

1. What are your wishes during normal labor and delivery?
2. How do you hope your baby will be treated immediately after birth and in the subsequent days?
3. What's the game plan in case of unexpected events?

And let's remember, some players choose a C-section even without complications.

Final level: Who's joining you in the delivery room? Got a contingency plan for complex births? How do you envision your newborn's initial care? Nail these, and you're game-day ready.

Packing the Perfect Hospital Bag

Transitioning from the dude who stared down a crib assembly manual to full-on Dad mode is no small feat. It's not just about showing up in the delivery room; it's about being all in—100% —ready to hold your partner's hand.

Childbirth? Intense? Understatement of the year. It's an intense emotional ride, bursting with excitement, and hey, a chance to rock those silly-looking scrubs.

Alright, future dads, real talk. The labor room isn't your DIY crib project—no winging it. You've got to come superhero-level prepared. Before our first child's arrival, my wife and I drafted a checklist for our hospital bag. About a month out, I was packing. Here's a peek:

- **For the Baby**: Diapers, wipes, a onesie, a possibly oversized hat, and other cute necessities. And a car seat —nope, babies can't Uber.
- **For the Mother**: Pads, extra outfits, and essentials you might be unfamiliar with—but they're vital. Yes, that includes nipple cream.
- **For Dad (That's You!)**: Basics like clothing, personal ID, insurance details, and snacks. Seriously, snacks. Maybe even a journal to jot down those spur-of-the-moment thoughts like contractions or sandwich recipes, who's judging?
- **General Awesomeness**: Toiletries, towels, sleepwear, flip-flops, the birth plan (got yours ready?), and for the love of the digital age, an extra-long charging cord. Go DJ mode? Bring a Bluetooth speaker.

No one-size-fits-all here. Collaborate with your partner, do your research, and maybe pick the brains of those experienced parents in your circle.

There you go, champ. Suited up and primed for the role of a lifetime. The next chapter's all yours. Embrace the whirlwind, keep a steady stride, and always remember. If you tamed that beastly crib assembly, you've got this whole parenting thing down. Go on and rock it!

What to Do When "It's Time"

You've heard about that magical moment when your kid inhales for the first time? Brace yourself. Witty comments and a poker face won't cover half of it. Let's drop the analogies. There's no playbook for the final stretch but chill out. You're not going solo on this.

Bet you've packed that hospital bag, huh? Good move! Less to stress about. Now, it's your turn to be the solid ground—just what your partner needs.

Now, labor stages? Imagine them as levels in a video game you've never played. Baffling? Yep. Manageable? Totally. Those jitters? Consider them your tutorial before the main event.

Be sharp on the labor signs. Don't mix them up with those fake-outs known as Braxton Hicks. Key signs to watch out for include:

1. Persistent lower back pain (Nope, not yours!)
2. Regular, short-interval contractions
3. The classic water break

At the hospital, I was everywhere. One second, I'm gripping her hand; the next, I'm the unofficial timekeeper. And then, the big moment—she pushes, I support, and boom, our baby's here. Grand finale? Snipping the cord is as monumental as cutting a ribbon at a grand opening.

When the limelight hits, and its action time, embrace the madness. Nervous? Awesome. Thrilled? Even better. Imagine playing the hero, the sidekick, and the joker in a show destined for rave reviews.

Fatherhood's not an act. It's reality at its best. Go out and nail it! Need a hand? Every dad's been there. We all made it, and you will, too. Welcome aboard!

SECTION 2: THE DELIVERY ROOM—A DAD'S PERSPECTIVE

Here is a story of a first-time dad (Sam) recollecting his day in the delivery room.

Walking into the delivery room felt overwhelming. It's one thing to read about it and another to live it. Seeing Stacey, determined yet weary, it dawned on me: this is real, and I'm in it.

Props to the medical staff—they were angels. My unending queries didn't faze them. They seemed to sense my internal tornado of anticipation and nervousness.

And then, Stacey's contractions. Again, hearing about them is different from witnessing and offering support. I did my bit with water, comfort, and, hopefully, the right words.

Our baby's arrival, with that heartwarming first cry, was surreal. There I was, scissors in hand, about to make the cut. Holding our baby, words just don't do it justice.

Delivery isn't a stroll in a park. It's an exhilarating blend of anxiety, happiness, and a cocktail of emotions. Blood? Yes. Complications? Maybe. But that's delivery in a nutshell.

Later, with our child snug against Stacey, I had a moment. The once intimidating room morphed into our family's starting point. It wasn't about the clinical vibe anymore; it was the birthplace of my new title: Dad.

It was also a reality check. This wasn't a single event but a start. The mélange of emotions hinted at the unpredictable adventure of parenting, and on that delivery day, everything just clicked.

Navigating Emotions, Supporting Your Partner, and Being Present

Alright, Dad, got your birth plan? Ace! Think of it as a cheat sheet for this epic baby journey. Hit the start button, and let's roll.

Here's how to weather this emotional storm, truly revel in it, and nail the whole "being there" gig for your partner. It's not about surviving but making the most of it.

This isn't just the beginning – it's the main event. Let's make some memories.

- **Understand the importance of support:** Your presence and support during labor can profoundly impact both the birthing person and the baby. Active engagement in the process can help your partner feel secure, promote quicker delivery, reduce the need for medical intervention, and improve bonding. It can also decrease the potential for the birth experience to be perceived as traumatic.

- **Provide emotional and practical support:** Your role in the delivery room is to provide emotional support, which looks different for each couple. Your partner may want a calming touch or massage, or she might prefer space. Understand your partner's needs and be prepared to meet them. Also, do not forget practical supports such as snacks, change for parking meters, or chargers for electronic devices.

- **Manage your reactions:** Stay calm and manage your expressions during labor and delivery. Maintaining a calm demeanor can help reassure your partner even if you feel anxious or stressed. Avoid showing horror, shock, or discomfort, as your partner might interpret these expressions negatively. Also, recognize and respect your limits. If you are uncomfortable with blood or medical procedures, make sure you position yourself in a place in the room that allows you to avoid seeing things you can't handle.

- **Understand the process and advocate:** Your role as an advocate means ensuring that your partner's wishes are respected during the birthing process. You should communicate with healthcare providers to meet your partner's needs in the delivery room.

- **Facilitate physical comfort and well-being:** One of the key roles you can play as a new dad in the birthing room is to facilitate your partner's physical comfort and well-being. This might include helping her change positions, walking with her, or assisting with breathing

32 | ULTIMATE DADS

exercises. You can also provide physical comfort by rubbing her back, holding her hand, or applying a cool compress to her forehead. You might want to bring items from home that could aid in relaxation, such as her favorite pillow, blanket, or scents. Additionally, be attentive to her hydration and nourishment needs, offering sips of water or bites of food when appropriate.

These are not the only tips that will push you through the delivery room and the moments after. Several tips and strategies may be unique to every pregnancy, making it imperative for you to be as engaged as possible.

Dealing With the Unexpected in the Delivery Room

Sometimes, no matter how well you plan, life tosses a wrench in the works. In those moments, a lot might rest on you. After all, your partner could be drained or out of it. That's why being clued in to tackle these curveballs is vital.

The following strategies should be your north star when things go south:

- **Be flexible**: Before delivery, you and your partner should realize that being flexible as you design that beautiful plan is essential. Pregnancy is a beautiful, chaotic experience; therefore, account for your desired birth plan but also consider the alternatives. There is a common adage that "Man plans, God laughs."

- **Communicate with your partner**: If your partner can still communicate effectively, engage them fully to arrive at a solution as quickly as possible.
- **Trust your medical team**: This moment reminds us that sometimes things are not in our control, and all we have to do is trust those well-equipped to manage the situation. As emotions rise and panic sets in, you may be tempted to give up on trust in your medical team, but this does not help the situation. Building trust and working collaboratively to ensure your baby and the mother are safe should be priorities.
- **Seek support**: Hey, more than ever, you need support from professionals and friends now. You can enlist the help of close friends or family members to ensure that you and your partner are surrounded by people who care about your well-being.
- **Be ready to adapt**: When the unexpected occurs, being prepared is critical. A change in the birth plan, an unanticipated medical intervention, or even a sudden shift in the baby's position could all be factors. Roll up your sleeves, don your problem-solving hat, and prepare to embrace Plan B (or C, or D... you get the picture).
- **Celebrate the miracles**: Regardless of the unexpected, keep your eyes open for the miracles that occur around you. Witnessing your child's birth is a magical, awe-inspiring experience. Allow joy and love to overcome any surprises that may arise. Remember, you are about to bring a new life into the world, which is pretty amazing.

You will handle unexpected twists and turns in the delivery room like a seasoned pro if you maintain a calm, flexible mindset, and a supportive attitude. And one day, you can tell your child a few epic stories about how they entered the world.

SECTION 3: BABY'S FIRST HELLO

Here is a recount of Luis's experience:

As the nurse gently placed my newborn son in my arms, I felt like a fish out of water. His tiny fingers reached out, curiously exploring the world, and I had no idea what he was reaching for. But I put my finger in that tiny hand, and he held on tight.

It was as if time stood still when our eyes locked, and all the noise and chaos of the delivery room faded away, leaving just the two of us in our little universe. His first hello was a silent message, a secret between a father and son, conveying a promise of unwavering protection and boundless love.

The Magic of Skin-To-Skin Contact and Bonding With Baby After Birth

"Research has shown that men who hold their baby close in the first 24 hours after birth report better bonding with their newborn. This is an essential and beautiful result of skin-to-skin contact" (Walsh, 2019, para. 5).

We're talking about skin-to-skin contact with your newborn, known as kangaroo care. Spoiler alert: It's even cooler than it sounds, and it's not just for moms – it's your ticket to the big leagues of fatherhood.

Imagine holding your mini-you, bare chest to bare chest. It's like an instant connection forged in love and possibly some spit-up. Goosebumps? Sure. Worth it? You bet it is.

Here's why this skin-time is more valuable than a playoff ticket.

- **Bonding boost**: It's like a superglue for emotional connections, thanks to hormones like oxytocin, aka "love hormone." This connection lays the groundwork for a bond stronger than your favorite team's defensive line.
- **Temperature control**: Your chest becomes a natural thermostat, keeping your baby snug while steadying their heart rate and breathing.
- **Immunity and chill**: Not only do you pass on your good bacteria to fortify your baby's immune system, but this proximity also dials down their stress levels. It's a win-win.
- **Pain relief and security**: you are their refuge in this alien world, lowering their pain perception and cradling them in safety.
- **Brain boost**: The sensory stimulation of skin-to-skin contact fires up their neural pathways and cognitive growth. It's like you are building the next Einstein.
- **Parenting perks**: Kangaroo care is a stress-buster for you, enhancing your caregiving confidence and giving you a "Heck yeah, I made this" moment.

Experience this skin-to-skin magic, pal. It lays the groundwork for a lifetime of love and nurturing. Trust me, it'll eclipse any game night memory. Except maybe that one time with the nachos, but we don't talk about that.

Tips for Your First Diaper Change

Get ready, you're about to embark on the thrilling ride of first-time diaper duty. I won't sugarcoat it – it's a bit like trying to put a genie back in the bottle after your first wish. But with a bit less magic and, well... you'll see.

That first diaper? I approached it with the grace of a moose trying to tiptoe. I remember glancing at the baby, wondering if they'd somehow already learned the eye-roll. Still, through all the mess (and boy, was there mess), it's a memory I cherish. Mostly.

Here's what I learned:

1. **Gather Your Gear**: Wipes, diapers, and maybe a hazmat suit. Oh, and a change of clothes for the baby. Maybe keep one on standby for yourself, just to be safe.
2. **Distraction Tactic**: It turns out babies are basically mini-Houdini's. Keep a toy or your singing voice handy. No judgment here; whatever gets you through.
3. **Fountain Alert**: If it's a boy... well, let's just say you might want to duck. It's the baby's version of a pop quiz, only wetter. And for the record, keeping them warm can help dodge that surprise.
4. **The Peekaboo Cleanup**: Lift, look, and wipe. Think of it as a less glamorous version of a magic trick.

5. **Diaper-Folding Mastery**: Those little tabs? They'll soon be less challenging than trying to get a word in with a toddler.

6. **Victory Dance**: Heck, why not? You've basically just tackled the baby version of an escape room. Take a moment to celebrate.

7. **Accept the Chaos**: Look, sometimes things get...unexpected. Laugh about it. You'll have more stories to swap at those inevitable dad meet-ups.

There you go, the straight poop. Before you know it, you'll be a diaper-changing master, advising the next set of puzzled-looking new dads.

Story: The First Dad-Baby Interactions and Their Impact (Luis aka "LA")

Standing in the nursery, holding my little guy, I remember feeling something that words almost can't describe. Our eyes met, and he made a sound that was half-question, half-statement, and I knew right then that things would never be the same again. The love, the responsibility – it was all real.

Now, being a dad is exhilarating. Here's the rundown.:

- **Leveling Up the Bond**: Those first connections are so pure and honest. The little things like a shared glance or a tiny hand grabbing your finger make you feel like you're part of something bigger. That's you and your child figuring each other out. Keep up the skin-to-skin contact.

- **Building the Trust Fortress**: They're so small, so trusting. You become their safe place when you're holding them, feeding them, or just being there. It's not a fortress of steel; it's a bond of love, care, and warmth that keeps them secure.
- **Unlocking Language Skills**: Babies love to hear your voice, whether you're reciting Shakespeare or just telling them about your day at work. How they look at you and try to make sense of those sounds is just priceless. And hey, if you sing off-key? They won't judge.
- **Mastering Dad Skills**: There'll be times when you feel like you're juggling flaming torches – like during the 3 AM feedings or that first time you're alone with the baby, and they decide it's meltdown o'clock. But you'll learn, adapt, and become more confident with every task.

Fatherhood is like walking into a room and forgetting why you came in, but instead of leaving confused, you leave with a baby in tow, equipped with a lifetime of new, exciting, and some-times messy adventures.

FATHERHOOD QUEST: THE FATHERHOOD EXPEDITION

If Chapter 1 was your introduction to the game, Chapter 2 is where the real adventure begins. You might be scratching your head, thinking, "Did I just hit the advanced level unexpectedly?" Mostly kidding. But on a serious note, gear up as we delve into the captivating world of your baby's grand entrance. And no, I'm not referencing fairy tale storks.

Level One: "Plan Architect."

Alright, quest one: Crafting the Birth Plan. This isn't akin to your childhood LEGO project, even if it sounds equally thrilling. It's the pivotal moment when you and your partner sit down to map out the vision for D-Day. Epidural considerations? Birthing ball? Midnight munchies? Get it all on paper, even if your scribbles look like hieroglyphics.

Level Two: "Serenity Guardian."

Welcome to the delivery room: the arena where life's most magical moment unfolds. It's comparable to the Super Bowl, except with more emotional touchdowns and perhaps fewer nachos. Your mission? Emanate tranquility. Offer a reassuring hand, be a comforting presence, and remember, staying conscious is a major bonus!

Level Three: "Newborn Welcomer."

Here it comes—the big reveal. You're about to be among the first to greet your little one. This isn't your average red carpet-event; it's the ultimate premiere. And here's a perk: babies aren't judgy. They won't mind the scruffy beard or the lingering aroma of last night's garlic pizza.

Level Four: "Moment Capturer."

Your new role? Family documentarian. Snap that inaugural picture or capture that first yawn on video. But here's a tip: Forget the quest for the perfect shot. This isn't a photoshoot; it's raw, real, and unfiltered. Just ensure the phone remains firmly in your grasp; babies aren't great catchers.

And there it is, aspiring dad. Ahead lies a path woven with awe, love, a sprinkle of uncertainty, and perhaps an unexpected splash or two. But here's the inside scoop: every step, stumble, and splash are worth it. I've trekked this path, and it's unforgettable.

Forge ahead and champion your unique dad journey. And a little wisdom to pocket: when it comes to loving and supporting your family, it's not about perfection but presence. Dive in with heart and soul.

Eager to glimpse what the first day as a dad holds? Gear up for revelations in the upcoming chapter!

3

DAY ONE—SURVIVING THE FIRST 24 HOURS AT HOME

Welcome to the big leagues, my friend! The first 24 hours at home with a newborn is like receiving a big, elaborate gift without an instruction manual. It's exciting, terrifying, and you're almost convinced there's a hidden camera somewhere.

You're now entering the 'fourth trimester.' Don't worry, no extra credit courses in parenthood here. It's just a fancy way of saying the first three months post-baby arrival. Oh boy, strap in!

Your newborn is like that friend who shows up to a party way too early and demands all the attention. I mean, they're adorable, but every two hours with the food demands? Come on, mini-me, pace yourself! And speaking of temperature control, their system's still working out the kinks, it's your job is to ensure they don't overheat or freeze. It's sort of like catering to a celebrity without Twitter followers.

Your partner is in the director's chair, recovering from the intense experience of childbirth or possibly a C-section while managing the never-ending cycle of breastfeeding. Even if you've elected to bottle feed, she's going to need you there, front and center, ready to tag in whenever required.

Skin-to-skin bonding between mom and baby? It's not just a tender scene; it's an essential one. It's where her body cues the orchestra to increase milk production (if that's the route she's taking) and wrap the baby in warmth and comfort. And those hormones she's dealing with? They're like the unpredictable weather on a movie set; they need time to get back on schedule.

It will be a three-month whirlwind of late nights, messy mishaps, and the kind of love you never thought you could feel. No understudies, no commercial breaks, just pure, unfiltered you-and-baby time.

Cue the applause, cue the tears and action! You've got this, and remember, when in doubt, changing a diaper is always easier than assembling anything from IKEA.

SECTION 1: WELCOME TO NO SLEEP CITY

Ah, sleep! Remember when that was a thing? Those were the days. Well, welcome to the Dad Club, where sleep becomes a myth; like that time, I thought I could build a treehouse without instructions (Spoiler: I couldn't).

But don't fret my bleary-eyed friend; you've joined the ranks of countless fathers who've navigated the mysterious land of No

Sleep City. Trust me, we've all been there and have the coffee stains to prove it.

Understanding Newborn Sleep Patterns

You've probably noticed your new VIP (Very Important Pooper) sleeps a lot but never when it's convenient for you? Welcome to the new dadhood, where your baby's sleep patterns are as predictable as my dance moves at a wedding.

Your little bundle of joy will be hitting the hay for 16–18 hours daily, but it comes in chunks that make you wonder if they're training for the Micro-Nap Olympics. You'll feel like Bill Murray in "Groundhog Day," but with fewer diapers and Andie MacDowell.

But here's the serious part (yes, even I get serious sometimes): sleep isn't just a hobby for your baby; it's their full-time job. It's where they grow, learn, and plot their next move to keep you on your toes. Your task? Ensure they get enough Z's, even if each nap seems as unique as... well, any word I try to spell without autocorrect.

Stay strong, keep laughing, and remember that adorable baby cuddles are your reward. I mean, who can resist those chubby cheeks? You've got this! And when in doubt, more coffee. Always more coffee.

Decoding Baby's Sleep Cues

Get ready to become a sleep detective because decoding your baby's sleep cues is a thrilling mission. It's like being on a secret mission, but instead of cracking codes, you'll be unlocking the secrets of your little one's slumber. Watch out for these telltale signs to know when your little one is feeling sleepy.

Babies give clear signals when they're feeling drowsy and need bedtime. Look for tiny yawns, gentle eye-rubbing, and increased fussiness. As sleepiness sets in, their activity level decreases, and they become quieter. Clenched fists, reduced eye contact, and fluttering eyelids indicate tiredness. Watch for slower, relaxed movements, and notice how cuddling or rocking can calm them into a peaceful slumber. Pay attention to these cues for a smoother bedtime routine.

Remember that every baby is unique, and their sleep cues might vary slightly. So, keep an eye out for these signs, and with time, you'll become a pro at knowing exactly when your little one is ready for a sweet slumber.

Balancing Night Duties With Your Partner

You're now in the magical realm of night duties, where your newborn's mysterious clock ticks to its own whimsical rhythm. But you've got your partner-in-crime, and you'll take on this new chapter like seasoned pros. Here's the game plan:

- **Open the Communication Channels**: First things first, talk it out. Really talk. Set some ground rules, divide, and conquer, and make sure you both know who's on duty when.
- **Craft Your Nighttime Strategy**: Whether it's taking turns or tag-teaming, find what makes your parenting duo harmonize. It's a bit like learning to dance with two left feet – at first.

- **Support Each Other's Sleep Quest**: If one of you looks like they've just run a marathon, step in, and give 'em a break.
- **Teamwork and Celebration**: Parenting's no solo mission. Rejoice in your little victories, even if it's just triumphing over a rebellious diaper.
- **Skip the Competition**: No keeping score unless it's counting laughs and smiles. You're in this thrilling ride together.
- **Plan Like a Pro**: Anticipate, prepare, execute. With a bit of foresight, you'll be one step ahead of the game.
- **Patience, Patience, and More Patience**: This isn't a sprint; it's a marathon. Support each other, learn together, and embrace the quirky adventure that is parenthood.

It might feel like uncharted territory right now, but trust me, you've got this! And if you ever feel in over your head, remember that the real heroes in life are those who rise every time they fall. Even if that rise involves a lot of caffeine. So, stay caffeinated, my friend!

Humorous Anecdotes About Misadventures Caused by Sleep Deprivation

Sleep deprivation in the first few days is a serious challenge for many parents, not just first-time parents. While sharing with a few of the parents about their misadventures because of sleep deprivation, our buddy Sam, a wildlife biologist, seemed to get hit harder (or was more willing to share), and we could not resist sharing them here.

The Lost Key Expedition

After a night filled with intermittent cries and comforting, I was set to take a peaceful drive to clear my head. I reached for the keys, only to find them missing. After what seemed like hours of searching, I discovered them in the refrigerator, next to the milk. Sleep deprivation had led me to this icy storage instead of the usual key hook. I had to chuckle at the situation; it was a harmless mistake but a vivid reminder that parenting can turn even the simplest tasks into complex puzzles.

The Grocery Store Odyssey

During a week of particularly broken sleep, I was responsible for picking up the week's groceries. My list was simple, but when I got to the store, I found myself wandering the aisles like a hunter lost in unfamiliar terrain. I filled the cart with everything but the essential baby formula. It was only when I returned home that I realized my mistake. My wife chuckled as I sheepishly headed back to the store.

Such incidents are a testament to the transformative nature of fatherhood, where the ordinary becomes extraordinary, and even seasoned veterans can find themselves humbled by the simplest tasks. It's all a learning experience, a chance to grow, and a reminder to take each day one step at a time, even if those steps occasionally lead us astray.

SECTION 2: CRY DECODER—UNDERSTANDING BABY'S LANGUAGE

The universal language of newborns is about to make its debut in your home. It's called crying, and it's like a music genre you didn't know you needed. Your tiny humans' vocalizations are their way of saying, "Hey, you there, there's an issue here!" It could be a tummy ache, the need for a bath, or just a position shift because, let's be honest, comfort is a luxury.

But don't worry; it's not a twisted game of parental torture. It's more like learning a new language through an immersive experience. Except this language comes with unique sound effects and no subtitles. Lucky for you, I'm here to help you decode these cries and guide you through the golden rules of baby understanding.

Deciphering Baby's Cries and What They Mean

Ah, fatherhood, you're just grabbing a warm cup of coffee, finally settling down, and then—BAM!—your little bundle of joy starts their solo concert. It's as if they know precisely when to cue the orchestra. My kid must have a sixth sense, or maybe it's just training to take over the world. Either way, I've learned to embrace the chaos with a grin and a shrug.

Now, about that crying? Those aren't just random noises; it's the language of baby town. Your mission, should you choose to accept it (and trust me, you don't have a choice), is to become fluent.

That wailing siren that makes you drop your coffee? It's not an emergency; it's lunchtime. The adorable yawn paired with a gentle cry? Bedtime's calling, and who wouldn't fall for that cuteness? Then there's the diaper-change jingle, and trust me, that one's unmistakable. And the pièce de résistance? The 'hold-me-right-now' ballad, which turns you into an instant super-hero. Not all heroes wear capes; some wear baby vomit.

Ready for the plot twist? A woman named Priscilla Dunstan says babies come with about five different vocal alarms. It's like Morse code but for babies. Now, get ready to crack the code, my friend. Parenthood's calling, and it's singing your name. Literally. In the most heart-melting way possible. Welcome to the chorus! You're in for a sweet, albeit slightly cacophonous, ride.

- *neh* = *"Dude, I'm starving!"*
- *owh* = *"Zzz-time incoming."*
- *heh* = *"Something's not right."*
- *eairh (sounds like someone stepped on a Lego)* = *"I've got some, uh, digestion issues."*
- *eh* = *"I need a good ol' burp."*

Once you've cracked this baby cry cipher, you're basically fluent in 'newbornese.' How's that for adding a new language to your resume?

The Golden Rules for Soothing a Crying Baby

Galen shared this with us:

Stepping into fatherhood, man, it's like stepping onto a new stage, where the spotlight is on this tiny human who's got you wrapped around their finger. Occasionally, that spotlight turns into a full-on siren. That was me, trying everything I knew to quiet my baby's cries, feeling a little out of my depth.

There I was, faced with a challenge. And challenges? I don't back down from them. I decided to sing, to give it everything, despite knowing that my voice might not win me any awards. I turned that living room into my arena and put on a show, not for fans or critics, but for the most important audience I've ever had.

And guess what? The crying stopped. Those little eyes looked up at me, maybe confused but intrigued. I could see that spark, that connection, and I felt like a rockstar. Not because I sang like one but because I reached my son in a way that nothing else had.

I may not be headlining concerts, but in that moment, I was every-thing to that little guy, and he was everything to me. We were connecting, really connecting, and those moments, those improvised lullabies, they became our thing, our way of bonding. And that's what fatherhood is all about: finding unique ways to create unforgettable connections with your child.

The first rule of Baby Club? Keep your cool. When that adorable mini-you decides to hold a mini-concert (and trust me, it'll happen), breathe. Remember, you're the cool director behind this blockbuster called parenthood. And your star? Well, they're just doing their own improv. Keep your calm, and they'll likely follow your lead.

Alright, let's dive into your toolkit. You've cracked the baby cry code, start by checking off the basics: are they hungry? Need a change? Just looking for snuggles? Swaddling them up might transport them back to their cozy womb days. A gentle sway? That's your go-to dance move now. White noise and lullabies? Think of them as the soundtrack to your new life. And if all else fails, a little groove with your baby to smooth tunes might do the trick. For bonus points, throw in a pacifier or a gentle baby massage. And when they need a distraction, break out those dad jokes in facial expression form or show them a mesmerizing object.

The world of baby soothing is vast. As you navigate it, you'll discover your own signature moves that hit the right note for your little co-star. Just remember, you've got this. Together, you two will figure out the perfect rhythm.

SECTION 3: NAVIGATING THE MESSY ADVENTURES —UNMASKING BABY POOP, DIAPER RASH MYSTERIES, AND SWADDLING

We're diving into the everyday joys of fatherhood: diapers, swaddling, and all the mysteries in between. Don't worry; you'll become an expert in no time. And by "expert," I mean you'll figure it out through trial and a whole lot of error.

Deciphering the Diaper: What's Normal and What's Not

Here's a basic rundown:

- **The First Poop**: It's dark and strange looking but perfectly normal. It usually occurs within 24 hours after the big entrance into the world. This debut number, known as meconium, resembles thick motor oil or something from a sci-fi movie. You'll get used to it.
- **Transitioning Colors**: Between days 2 and 4, the sequel takes a lighter tone, literally. From dark green to an

optimistic yellow/green, and finally to a gentle tan or mustard yellow, kind of like a mood ring but less fun.

- **Breast Milk vs. Formula**: Breastfed babies prefer to keep things soft and seedy. In contrast, formula fans go for the firmer, more peanut butter-esque approach. Either way, expect various textures. It's just part of the job.

- **The Shades of Brown**: Yep, lots of them. You might feel like a paint mixer at a hardware store. With formula-fed stars, you get a rich palette of brown, ranging from yellow-brown to green-brown. It carries a more robust fragrance, somewhere between a bouquet of roses and, well, poop.

- **Diaper Changing Again:** Feel like you're reliving the same scene over and over? Welcome to the loop of endless diaper changing. Spoiler alert: it's utterly normal! But, like any good series, there will be new seasons and evolving requirements. Stay tuned.

- **Something Seems Off:** Call the pediatrician if there are unexpected changes in the frequency or appearance or if there's a sudden dramatic turn with fussiness.

How to Handle Diaper Rashes

Diaper rashes vary in intensity, ranging from mild to severe. You may observe small pink or red spots or patches on your baby's bottom in mild cases. In contrast, in more severe situations, the spots might appear even brighter red, and the skin may display signs of cracking, breaking, or blistering. Additionally, the rash could extend down to the legs or up the abdomen, and your little one might exhibit signs of discomfort, such as crying or distress (Sweeney, 2020).

Diaper rash: it happens. Here's how to deal with it:

- **Keep Things Clean**: Just like washing your hands, tidy that changing area.
- **Use a Good Cream**: Find and stick to a brand you trust. Your baby will thank you.
- **Pick the Right Diaper**: Opt for a gentle-on-the-skin choice, there's no need to overthink it.
- **Give it Air**: Sometimes, bare is best. Just watch for those surprise "accidents."
- **Avoid Harsh Products**: Stick to gentle wipes, like you'd use sensitive skin soap for yourself.
- **Still a Problem?:** Time for professional advice from the pediatrician.

Becoming a dad isn't about having all the answers right away. It's about learning as you go, just like assembling that crib without the instructions (not that I'd recommend that). There's no perfect way to diaper or swaddle, but there is your way. You'll find what works for you and your baby with a bit of patience and probably a few messes. And that's really what it's all about.

Embrace the chaos, the mess, and the mystery of it all. You're doing great. Even if it doesn't always feel like it, you're precisely the dad your little one needs. Now, back to those diapers— you've got this!

Swaddling 101: Why It Helps and How to Become a Swaddling Pro

Let's chat about swaddling. You've probably heard of it, and if you're anything like me, it sounds a bit like a thing only baby experts or grandmothers know how to do. But here's the deal—it's not that complicated, and it's your ticket to a (hopefully) calmer baby.

Think of swaddling like wrapping a burrito; only this burrito wiggles and occasionally cries. The goal? Recreate the womb's coziness. Here's a step-by-step breakdown:

1. **Arms up**: Wrap one corner of a soft blanket across your baby's chest. It's like they're about to give you a high five. Except, you know, they can't do that yet.
2. **Bottom-up**: Fold the bottom corner and tuck it securely behind your baby. This is the part that keeps their feet warm.
3. **Arms down**: Wrap the other corner around them, arms down like a baby burrito hug.

Give their legs room to move, and if they start rolling over, it's time to say goodbye to swaddling. Remember that swaddling is ideal for sleep or when your baby requires soothing comfort. Allow those little arms and legs to roam free during the day for exploration and development.

FATHERHOOD QUEST - THE DAD SKILL-ATHLON

It's like the Olympics but with less fanfare and more diapers. Here's how you level up:

Level 1 - Newbie Night Owl!

Survive three nights in a row, waking up at least twice to soothe the baby without hitting snooze. Coffee is your friend, and sleep is overrated anyway.

Level 2 - Cry Decoder:

Decode five different cries in a single day, using only your newfound dad's intuition. Hunger? Sleepy? Time for a cuddle? Who needs a manual when you've got those finely tuned dad ears? Your detective badge awaits.

Level 3 - Change Champ!

Successfully change five diapers in one day without a hitch. No mess, no fuss, no phone-a-friend. You're in the big leagues, equipped with wipes, creams, and that unmistakable glow of diaper victory.

This fatherhood thing? It's not always glamorous. It's messy, exhausting, and filled with surprises. But hey, you're nailing it. And even when you feel like you're not, remember: your baby thinks you're the most incredible person in the room, even with that spit-up on your shirt. You've got this!

Diving into Chapter 4, you might want to sit down for this. Your tiny human is about to pull off a number of significant stunts in just a month. Doubling in weight? Check. Flashing that grin that's a total heart-melter? Absolutely. Brace yourself – it's a month of jaw-dropping baby feats coming right up.

4

MONTH ONE—THE SEA OF CHANGE

Your touch? It's not just comforting; it's like a brain-building superpower. By eight weeks, you're practically a mind-molder, shaping that tiny brain with love and care.

Now, let's talk about the first month. It's like the world's cutest rollercoaster, filled with tiny toes and smiles that'll steal your heart faster than you can say "diaper rash."

Right, Dad, I'm about to drop some science on you. This whole "breast milk appears out of nowhere" phenomenon isn't as mysterious as it sounds. Before your baby's grand entrance, the mom's body is busy prepping for breastfeeding, with a little enhancement in the chest region. Once the little one starts to latch on, it's like hitting the play button on the hormones, and there's milk. Just like that, your tiny superstar's set up with the ultimate meal plan. No fuss, no muss. Welcome to the magic show.

Understanding the Basics of Breastfeeding

Breastfeeding is like unlocking that ultimate bonus level for your baby. It's a supercharged smoothie of everything incredible—perfect nutrition, immune level-ups, and a special mom-baby connection bonus that makes other power-ups look like they're playing in the minor leagues. Consider it the best opening move in your child's game of life.

As a first-time dad, you might have many questions about breastfeeding. We've got your back, addressing the most common queries to help quell your jitters.

Let's face it; you're not equipped with the in-game milk perk—big deal. Don't underestimate your Player 2 capabilities. Your role? Unwavering support. No milk on tap? No problem! You are the ace of bottle feeding. Enjoy those precious father-child bonding moments, whether it's pumped breast milk or formula.

Sleep? Oh, you mean that elusive legendary item that no one seems to have any more? A bit of planning and strategy with the night feedings can turn that myth into reality. Think of it as unlocking a secret level of rest.

Breastfeeding is not always smooth sailing, but remember, even superheroes face hitches. Patience and support are your trusty sidekicks. Cheer your partner on and if needed, get expert help (lactation consultant) and be her constant co-pilot on this journey.

Here's where you shine, Dad. Offer a helping hand, use your kind words, or simply keep things calm. It's not just mom's job

—it's teamwork. Together, you'll make this a beautiful experience for your little one. GG, Dad. GG.

The Role of a Dad in the Breastfeeding Journey

It's not just about being there; it's about being involved. Support, comfort, and a helping hand with positioning or burping the baby can make all the difference. You're part of this team, and your role is pivotal.

An Introduction to Formula Feeding: When, Why, and How

Here's the deal, straight from the dad's guide to being awesome: Formula feeding is like your dependable friend who's always there when you need him. It offers flexibility for the mom, permits shared feeding responsibilities, and ensures the baby's nutritional needs are met even if breastfeeding is impossible. It's also handy for those who face lactation challenges or juggle a hectic schedule. Every family's got its rhythm – the main gig is to keep the baby thriving and the home team smiling.

- Consider your baby's nutritional needs first and check the ingredients! Does the little one got food quirks? There's a blend for that.
- Getting it right is like fine-tuning a recipe. Aim for that perfect body temperature (98.6°F or 37°C). Test it out like a pro chef – a few droplets on your wrist or the back of your hand should feel like a warm handshake from a friend, not a sizzling high-five from a stovetop.
- Hygiene? Treat that bottle like it's hosting royalty— sterilize it like the Queen is coming for tea.

- And finally, watch the serving size because babies can go for the whole buffet or just an appetizer.

And those bonding moments? They're still there. Maintain eye contact, switch sides, and remember, whether it's breast milk or formula, you're providing more than just food—you're building a connection.

Personal Story: Meet Nick

Here is an amusing narrative by fellow dad Nick about his breastfeeding experiences.

As a rookie dad, I approached breastfeeding with the confidence of a turkey on Thanksgiving. My wife struggled with our newborn's latching. In my desperation, I Googled "baby not latching." One piece of advice said, "Squish the nipple like a sandwich." I shared this nugget of wisdom with my wife. She laughed so hard our little tyke latched onto her mid-giggle! The nipple sandwich trick worked, just not as expected!

SECTION 2: BONDING WITH BABY IN THE FIRST MONTH

Wow, the first month with your baby. It's like opening a gift that poops. But it's not just about changing diapers and figuring out how those tiny onesies work. It's a month filled with bonding, and here's how you pull off that magic without needing to consult a wizarding manual.

The Power of Touch

Okay, you know how moms have this incredible, almost supernatural connection with their babies? Dads have that, too, but ours comes with a "cool" vibe.

Let me tell you about my buddy Lawrence. We were hanging out one day, diving into the deep end of fatherhood topics—specifically, the weight that a dad's touch can carry. (Bear with me; this will all connect, I promise.)

Every time I walk through that door after work, I make it a point to give my daughter a quick back rub. It's become our thing, our little ritual. She even calls me out if I forget.

I grew up in a home where affection was as rare as a blue moon. I never saw my dad so much as give my mom a hug. But then, this incredible thing happened on my graduation day. My dad came up to me, patted my back, and told me he was proud. It was like hitting an emotional jackpot. It wasn't just his words—it was the power in that simple touch. That's why I make sure to share that same magic with my daughter; I understand its worth.

Lawrence's story hits home the monumental influence a dad's touch can have in shaping a child's world. It's a wake-up call, spotlighting that small, everyday gestures of love can wield a mighty force in forging tight-knit connections between fathers and their kids. It's not always about grand actions or poetic words; at times, the most potent messages come from the simplest touches.

According to a super scientific 2020 article in The Brussels Times (yes, I did my homework), physical touch from parents does all kinds of fancy things, like calming heart rhythms and helping with a baby's body recovery. Think of it as giving your child a big, warm, physiological hug with science.

Bottom line: Your touch is golden. It's akin to draping your newborn in a superhero cape. Every snug, cuddle, or affectionate peck? It's your silent vow of "I've got you" in their brand-new world.

Understanding the Science of Skin-To-Skin Contact

Modern dads aren't just in the waiting room. They're in the thick of baby action. The University of South Australia introduced "kangaroo care"— not about hopping marsupials, but pure skin-to-skin cuddling. It's akin to being their cozy human pouch, replicating the womb's warm embrace.

When you and baby strip down to basics, here's the magic that unfolds:

- **Good Vibes Only**: Your touch is their VIP ticket.
- **Zen Mode**: Think of it as a spa day, just minus the fancy robes.
- **Inbuilt Warmth**: Who knew you doubled up as a toasty wrap?
- **Microbial Bodyguards**: Your skin preps baby's defenses.
- **Synced Rhythms**: Your beats align, bridging hearts.

In short, dads aren't just spectators anymore. You're the co-pilot, the roadie, and the fan club president. Buckle in (or maybe that's strap on the baby carrier?) for the ultimate bonding adventure. Isn't evolution incredible?

Mastering the Skin-to-Skin Connection

Ready for the Chief Snuggler badge? Here's the drill:

- Post-birth: Go shirtless. Hold tight. Welcome to the dad club.
- Locate the comfy zone.
- Nudie Time: Babies? Zero judgments.
- Stay zen.
- Gaze magic: Speak without words.
- Decode baby cues.
- Patience: It's not a race.
- Opt for quality snuggles.
- Loop in your partner.
- Make it a ritual.

Wrapping up, dads are in the spotlight. You're the co-captain, the backstage manager, and the top fan. Get ready to wrap up for this heartwarming journey. Evolution? It's a beaut!

Meet Logan

The delivery room is when everything hit home. When they handed me my baby and our skin touched, I knew things would never be the same. It wasn't flashy, but it was love, pure and unfiltered.

Fast forward a few weeks, and I'm coming home from work and looking forward to having "our time." Every evening, holding my little one became the highlight of my day. Nighttime feedings became less about feeding and more about bonding. Just having my baby close, feeling that little heartbeat, made even the longest workday worth it.

As the weeks turned into months, things got even better. My baby began to recognize me, and suddenly, those smiles weren't just reflexes - they were for me. We connected, not with words, but with something more profound. Every morning, that smiling face was my reward.

Sure, there were tough nights when sleep seemed like a distant dream. But even then, holding my baby, feeling those tiny fingers, was all it took. It was a simple act that worked wonders.

And as time went on, I realized that these moments weren't just about soothing my child; they were about our connection. Each touch, each smile, was a reminder of a connection growing daily.

By the time the first three months had passed, those simple moments of skin-to-skin contact had become our foundation. It wasn't about grand gestures but love, trust, and our shared journey. And as the days continue to go by, I know that this bond, formed through the simplest of touches, will stay with me forever.

That's what being a dad has been for me. It is not a series of significant, dramatic events but a collection of small, perfect and not so perfect moments that have added up to an extraordinary experience. It's not just a role; it's a relationship. And it's one I wouldn't trade for anything.

SECTION 3: THE MAGIC OF THE DADDY VOICE

The best way to coax a baby into saying her first words? Talk, talk, and talk some more.

— -WEISS

We're diving into the mysterious realm of Dad's voice—a tool that's more magical than a Swiss Army knife at a camping trip, yet completely underrated. Ready? Let's crank this up.

Your voice is a superpower that captivates your baby's attention. From heartwarming lullabies to animated storytelling, you can create a world of wonder through the sound of your voice. Let's explore your voice's extraordinary impact on your little one, fostering a bond that will resonate for a lifetime.

The Impact of a Dad's Voice on a Newborn's Development

Ever notice how you can talk to your baby, and suddenly, they're listening like you're the most fascinating thing in the room? That's the magic of a dad's voice. Even if your singing makes people cringe, it's the best sound for your newborn.

From their first day, your voice is a guide and comfort. And those dad jokes you've been saving? Now's the time. Trust me; they'll never have a more appreciative audience.

Go on, embrace your inner superstar. Whether telling tales of knights and dragons or asking them if they've got your nose, your voice is the golden ticket. The stage is set, and you're the headliner.

Ideas for Talk-Time with Your Baby: Reading, Singing, and Narrating

We've chatted about bonding with your kiddo when they're still kicking around inside the womb, but let's be honest—the real fun starts once they've checked into the world. You've got this new baby, and it's time to have fun. Here are a few simple and everyday ways to engage:

- **Storybook Adventures**: Grab a picture book. There is no need for a grand adventure; your voice will take them there.
- **Nonsensical Tunes**: Who cares if you can't sing? Your baby thinks you're terrific.
- **Freestyle Fairytales**: Make something up. You've got this.
- **Day-in-the-Life Narrations**: Talk them through breakfast or changing a diaper. It's surprisingly engaging.
- **Splish-Splash Serenades**: Baths can be fun, especially with a bit of singing.
- **Morning Jingles**: Why not start the day with a little song?
- **Bust-a-Move Dance Party**: Dance with your baby. They won't judge your moves.
- **Animal Noise Fiesta**: Everyone loves animal noises. Right?

- **Baby Banter**: They coo, you coo back. It's a great conversation.

Here's a neat trick: your voice can calm your baby down. Talk softly, sing a little, or hum a tune. They know your voice and find it comforting.

There you have it: a menu of fun, laughter, and a connection that starts now and doesn't have an expiration date. Enjoy the journey, fellow adventurer. The road's filled with wonder, and you're driving the car.

Using Your Voice to Soothe Your Baby

Pop quiz time. What's a new parent's secret weapon? No, it's not that coffee IV drip (though, believe me, it's a close second). It's that smooth vocal styling of yours. That voice of yours? It's like a big bear hug but in sound waves. When your tiny human is having a meltdown, your voice is like the world's best chill pill. Those gentle whispers and lullabies work better than any bedtime story, whisking them off to the land of sweet dreams.

Your voice isn't just today's comfort—it's a blast from their past. We're talking way back when they were doing the butterfly stroke in the womb. To them, you're the original soundtrack of life. When storms of cries hit, you're the safe harbor they sail to.

Feeling like a rockstar yet? Good, because it doesn't stop there.

The Positive Long-Term Effects of Verbal Interaction with Your Baby

When you're babbling back at your baby or narrating your epic (or not-so-epic) day, you're investing in their future. Consider it an early deposit into their "Life Skills" account. Research shows that babies who experience rich verbal interaction tend to have larger vocabularies, better language skills, and enhanced cognitive abilities as they grow (Yang et al., 2021). More words now mean a head start in vocab, sharper language skills, and a turbocharged brain ready for all the learning curves ahead.

As your baby grows, they mimic your sounds and eventually form their first words. Your verbal engagement sets them on the path to becoming confident communicators.

And here's the big finish: those chit-chats aren't just brain boosters. They're soul food. You're building trust, understanding, and empathy. Those early gab sessions pave the way for a lifetime of meaningful relationships.

Keep talking, singing, and maybe even throw in a little dance move now and then. You're not just entertaining; you're molding the future—one coo, lullaby, and dad joke at a time. Your vocal cords have never been more vital, my friend. Rock on with your bad self.

FATHERHOOD QUEST: FEEDING FRENZY

Game on, dads! Prepare yourself for the ultimate Fatherhood Quest. And trust me, these levels are way cooler than any video game you've ever played (and, you know, with fewer dragons). Brace yourself, and let's unlock these dad achievements!

Level 1: Midnight Milk Sommelier

Be the ultimate wingman during breastfeeding marathons. Nail those perfect positioning techniques and come equipped with pillows and water like a pro butler. The idea? Keep Mom in her A-game.

Level 2: Formula Mixmaster

Who needs a bartender when you can be a formula connoisseur? Perfect that formula recipe—measure, mix, and serve up a bottle warm and delightful enough to make any 5-star chef jealous.

Level 3: Burp Maestro

Rise to the challenge of mastering the elusive baby burp. Your goal? Gentle pats, soothing vibes, and the most satisfying baby burps this side of anywhere. It's like a mini applause for your expert feeding assistance.

Level 4: Night Owl Extraordinaire

Embrace the night by manning the nocturnal feedings for a week straight. Showers of appreciation (and maybe an actual shower) await as you bolster Mom and baby through the darkest hours. Who needs sleep when you're on a quest?

Here we are, hitting Chapter 5. Think of our parenting journey like a stroll through the supermarket. At times, you're cruising the snack aisle, and other times, you find yourself lost in the home cleaning section, wondering why you need seventeen varieties of bleach.

Each growth spurt our kiddo hits is like discovering they've moved the cereal again. Surprise! But don't worry, we're not just here to endure the messy spills and temper tantrums in aisle three. We're in this to enjoy those unexpected "Hey, they finally like broccoli!" moments.

It is a great time to grab your shopping list and fasten your seatbelt, which is probably covered in crackers and mystery stains (just like your favorite dad shirt). We're about to explore the next significant milestones with our little one. And who knows? We might even find that elusive perfect avocado. Ready to wheel down the aisles with me?

5

MONTH 3—THE SMILES AND GIGGLES

Three months in, and here we are! You've survived sleepless nights and are rewarded with giggles that can turn even the gloomiest day around. Now, it's the catchy soundtrack of your life.

SECTION 1: ENGAGING WITH YOUR BABY

At three months, it's time to get to know your baby. They're curious, and it's not just about feeding and changing anymore. They want to play, and you're their favorite playmate. From peek-a-boo to funny faces, it's about spending quality time together. Imagine catching up with an old friend—only this one's much smaller and cuter.

Understanding the Importance of Early Stimulation and Interaction

Here's where it gets real. How you talk, play, and interact with your baby lays the foundation for everything to come. You're not just entertaining them; you're teaching them about the world. And no, you don't need a teaching degree, just a willingness to be there and be involved.

Think of your baby's brain as the latest smartphone without the monthly bill. Now, you're the one installing the coolest new apps on it. This isn't coding; it's more like loading it with fun games, catchy tunes, and quality dad content.

Here is a Pro Tip from Matt: Start conversing with your baby. Talk to your baby like they're your co-pilot in this journey. Share the big thoughts, the little ones, the weird ones. They're listening, and they love the sound of your voice even more than you love that latest binge-watch.

The big takeaway? In a nutshell? It's not about crafting the perfect parenting playbook but showing up and dialing into their frequency.

Fun and Simple Activities to Bond With Your Baby

Ready to step up your game? Here are a couple easy ways to bond:

- **Baby Massage**: It's like a prolonged, gentle hug that's soothing for both.
- **Storytime**: More than words, it's sharing a moment with your voice as the only narration.

- **Tummy Time**: An exploration together, not just hitting milestones.
- **Dance Party**: Who cares about dance moves? Put on your favorite song and enjoy the rhythm together.
- **Peek-a-Boo**: It's a classic for a reason. It's not just a game; it's a lesson in trust and joy.
- **Sensory Play**: Let them explore textures and shapes. An adventure right in your living room.
- **Baby Sling Strolls**: A walk together can be more than exercise; it's a chance to show them your world.
- **Face Fun**: Your expressions teach them how to express themselves. Pure communication at its core.
- **Finger Painting**: Less about the art, more about the messy, memorable experience.

Parenting isn't a performance; it's a journey. These activities aren't chores; they're opportunities to grow together. Dive in, explore, laugh, and learn together. They won't be this small forever; every day is a new opportunity to make memories. It's the actual work, the good work, and you're just the person for the job.

Dev and His Baby

Starting out as a father, I must admit there was a lot of uncertainty. Questions were filling my mind, but the minute I held my baby girl, Zahra, all that doubt just vanished. In that instant, something changed, it clicked, and I knew a connection was born that I would never break.

You know, fatherhood pushes you to try new things. There I was, finding this baby yoga class while I was on paternity leave, yeah it was a little early, but you can start yoga when the baby is 6 weeks old, so I thought 'what the heck.' Was I out of my element? Sure. But man, connecting with Zahra through those stretches, hearing her laugh - it became our thing. We weren't just showing up; we became the heart of that class. Seeing her smile was a feeling that made me proud and made me feel like I was doing okay.

Music's always been special, and it was just natural to start strumming my guitar for her. Those lullabies, those moments where she'd just look at me with those big eyes, they became our time, our daily ritual. It's more than just notes; it's a connection.

Weekends were our time for fun and magic. We'd turn the living room into a fort, going on adventures together, just me and her. It's those simple things, you know? Those are the memories.

And as she grew, I realized we were in this together. Her taking her first steps, I saw us walking this journey side by side. Challenges? They were just chances to grow closer and understand each other more.

Here's what I've learned: It's about being there, really being in the moment. It's about loving and showing that love in the small things. It's baby yoga, it's those sweet melodies, it's playtime. But more than that, it's about building something unbreakable, something that's going to last. It's me and Zahra, father, and daughter, connected at the heart for life.

SECTION 2: DECIPHERING BABY'S SLEEP

Deciphering a baby's sleep? Think of it as a constantly evolving puzzle where each night, just when you think you've got it, there's a whole new set of clues (and perhaps a few more cups of coffee). But each night, you learn a little more, grow a little closer, and become that much better at the most rewarding puzzle.

Recognizing Baby's Sleep Patterns and Challenges In Month 3 and Beyond

Hey there, future sleep expert! You know, cracking the code of your baby's sleep patterns is kind of like trying to complete a challenging puzzle level without a guide. You managed the newborn patterns, and now there this new stage with another mystery on your hands. Honestly, it feels like your little one is channeling their inner game master.

Cues and Signals: Keep an eye out for those telltale signs like yawning and eye-rubbing. It's like your baby's version of a "low battery" warning, and they might just be ready to hit the save point and take a nap.

The Sleep Challenges: These are the plot twists of parenting. Sleep regressions, teething, early risings—it's like navigating a tricky maze. But remember, there's always a way out, and you've got a whole team ready to back you up. Reach out to family, friends, or even online groups.

For many, consistency may seem like the lesser thrill in the rollercoaster of parenting, but here's the twist. Remember that bedtime routine you've been establishing? Consider it akin to a gamer setting a strategy to conquer a pivotal boss level. Whether it's a story, a lullaby, or simply dimming the lights, they're not just nightly rituals, they're combo moves that lead your child seamlessly into the land of dreams.

Now, let's conquer a few common sleep challenges:

- **Night Wakings:** At times, when your little one wakes up during the night, think of it not as a setback but as a surprise "Pause" in your game of parenting. Just like in gaming, it's not about the interruptions but how you react to them. With consistent naps and well-established bedtime routines, you're well-equipped to face fewer night-time disruptions.
- **Sleep Regressions**: Ah, the dreaded sleep regressions! In the world of parenting, these can feel like unexpected difficulty spikes in your game. But remember, like any seasoned gamer, adapting to the situation and sticking to your routine is the key to navigating these challenges. It's not about never facing a hiccup; it's about how you continue the journey afterward.
- **Teething Troubles**: When those first teeth start making an appearance, it can feel like you've encountered a mini-boss battle. But much like in games, there are power-ups available. Teething toys, massages, and the like are your special moves to soothe those gums and secure a win. Oh, and look up teething ties – no seriously, look it up.

- **Early Rising**: Do you have an early riser? Think of it as a game setting that needs a little tweak. The solution can be as simple as equipping your nursery with blackout curtains. In the grand game of parenting, these might just be your secret cheat code to prolonged sleep.
- **Dream Feeding**: This might sound like a strategy straight out of a fantasy game, but trust us, it's all real. Gently waking your baby for a feed just before you head to bed can result in a longer, more restful sleep for both of you. It might seem counterintuitive, but it's a tactic worth considering in the quest for sleep. This technique championed by baby sleep experts, such as renowned author and pediatrician Dr. Harvey Karp, is a clever little trick that might just help you and your baby catch extra zzzs.

Let's delve into a sample schedule to help paint a clearer picture. (Just keep in mind that you should try this around the three-month mark.)

6:30 p.m.: Nourishing meal before their first sleep of the night.

7 p.m.: Tuck your baby into bed.

10 p.m.: Gently rouse your baby without fully waking them and give them a late-night feed.

4 a.m.: Just like clockwork, your little one stirs for a feeding.

7 a.m.: Your baby awakens, ready for a fresh day filled with new experiences.

Be flexible and willing to adjust your approach as needed. Most importantly, be kind to yourself. Sleep issues are a natural part of parenting, and you are doing a fantastic job, even when things get tough.

SECTION 3: BABY-PROOFING YOUR RELATIONSHIP

Door locks and electrical sockets might come to mind when you think of babyproofing. But what about safeguarding the most essential thing amidst baby chaos – your relationship with your partner? This is the most significant and rewarding quest.

Navigating Changes in Your Relationship Post-baby

Fantastic, you've baby-proofed every nook and cranny, but what about relationship-proofing? Baby-proofing isn't just for sharp corners; it's also about adjusting your relationship to embrace this new phase of life.

- **Acceptance**: Recognize that things have changed.
- **Patience**: Understand that adapting takes time.
- **Communication**: Discuss your feelings and concerns.
- **Teamwork**: Parenting is a joint venture.
- **Time Out**: Spend quality time as a couple, not just parents.
- **Balance**: Share responsibilities fairly.
- **Empathy**: Step into each other's shoes now and then.
- **Solo Side Quests**: Don't forget those individual missions, even in the chaos of baby duties. Enjoy a good book, a jog, or even a favorite game—these respites are like secret levels for your sanity.

Change is like a game update: unexpected and occasionally challenging, but it makes the game more interesting. Why not dance in the kitchen, laugh at the mess, back each other up, and embrace the new co-op parenting mode. You're not just partners; you're a dynamic duo, ready to tackle this beautiful, chaotic expansion pack called parenthood.

Maintaining a Strong and Healthy Relationship

Bringing a baby into the world can feel like trying to assemble intricate furniture without an instruction manual. It's a challenge, but with the right tools (communication, patience, and understanding), you can keep your relationship intact and strengthen it.

- **Team Up Like You Mean It**: You're in this together, think of yourselves as a dynamic duo. Divide, conquer, laugh at the mess, and high-five over those tiny victories. Your love story is now an adventure, and every adventure needs a strong team.
- **Speak Your Heart, Not Just Your Mind**: Communication is the Wi-Fi of love. Share the weird, the wonderful, and the worrisome. Being transparent is the core of a strong relationship.
- **Date Nights**: Now with 50% More Sweatpants: Remember romance? Yeah, it's still a thing. Plan those dates, even if it's on the living room floor, surrounded by toys. Talk, reconnect, and maybe, just maybe, forget about baby stuff for a while.
- **Gratitude is an Attitude**: A little "thank you" goes a long way. Celebrate each other's triumphs, even the

diaper-related ones. Every little gesture is a gold star on the partner's report card.

- **Bend, Don't Break**: Plans will change. Diapers will explode. Babies will cry. Flexibility is a vital relationship skill. Roll with the punches and laugh off the chaos.
- **Self-Care Isn't Selfish**: Encourage each other to pursue those hobbies, even if it's a five-minute walk to the mailbox. Taking care of you makes you better at taking care of each other.
- **Create Your Own Rituals**: Whether it's pancake Sundays or a dance-off before bedtime, make memories that are uniquely yours. These traditions will be like inside jokes that keep you bonded through thick and thin.
- **Keep the Spark Alive But Mind the Baby Monitors**: Intimacy doesn't have to be a blockbuster romance scene. It's the hugs, the knowing glances, and those random kisses. Keep it alive, even if it's in snippets.

You two are the rock stars of this new family band, and how you play together sets the tone for everything. With a bit of love, laughter, and the occasional off-key solo, you'll not only hit the right notes but create a symphony that's entirely your own.

Jerry's Tale

Our lives got flipped, filled with love and joy, when that little one came into the picture. But hey, nobody handed us a manual on how to deal with the 3 a.m. cries, the diapers, and those moments where we just couldn't see eye to eye. Our connection, which we thought was great, started to show some cracks. We were tired, grumpy, lost, and our relationship was on the edge.

But you know what? Love's a powerful thing, and it helped us find our way back. We started to talk, really talk, about what was going on inside. We opened up, not afraid to show our fears and our struggles. We began to see that this journey of parenthood was new for both of us, and that we had to face it together. Our love for our kid and each other was too strong to let go.

We learned to dance in the rain, finding joy in those crazy, messy parenting moments. We kept the fire alive with date nights, even if it was just on the couch with takeout. We reminded ourselves to take a breather, to look after ourselves so we could be there for each other.

And guess what? With time, love, and a lot of patience, we started to harmonize again. We found strength in our imperfections, growing closer through the highs and lows.

Parenthood? It's not a walk in the park, but it's our journey, and we're walking it together. We've got something solid and real; no challenge will break that.

FATHERHOOD QUEST: BOND (NOT JAMES BOND)

Level 1: Baby Talk: The Language of Love (and Confusion)

Master the fine art of "babyese." It's all coos, gurgles, and interpretive dances. If all else fails, smiling and nodding is a universal language.

Level 2: The Work-Home Juggle: A Circus Act Without the Tent

Balance work, home, and baby like an Olympic gymnast—with less grace and more spilled milk. Remember, if you can't find your phone, it might be in the fridge.

Level 3: The Baby Gear Gauntlet: Gadgets, Gizmos, and Why is This So Complicated?

Assemble the stroller without losing your sanity or exhausting your swear jar. And yes, duct tape is considered a legitimate tool.

Level 4: Date Night at Home: The Ultimate Power-Up

Plan and execute a date night at home that makes takeout feel like fine dining and the living room like a five-star restaurant. Bonus level unlocked if you can do it without waking the baby. This power-up not only refills your romance meter but gives you and your partner the energy boost needed to face another round of parenting. Game on!

There you have it, fatherhood tasks that come with all the fun and chaos of parenting. It's like a game show, but the prizes are measured in baby smiles and moments of peace and quiet. Happy questing!

6

MONTH SIX—HERE COMES TROUBLE

Hey, Dad, fasten that baby-proof seatbelt of yours because the rollercoaster of parenting is about to hit a chaotic circuit! Do you think you've got the hang of this dad thing? Cute. But here comes Chapter 6 of "Here Comes Trouble," and your tiny roommate is ready to spice things up.

SECTION 1: WELCOME TO MOBILITY—ROLLING AND CRAWLING

Oh, you wanted a calm, stationary baby? Adorable. Now's the time when your living room turns into an obstacle course, and your child becomes an aspiring gymnast.

Understanding the Start of Mobility and Its Implications

It's incredible, you turn your back for one second, and suddenly, your baby performs a complete 180 and is off on a grand adventure. That's right; your very own mini-Houdini has learned to roll over. Next up, crawling, and it's not the military type, though that would be quite a sight.

These tiny movements may seem small but huge in the parent world. They're akin to a baby's first steps toward conquering the world (or at least the living room). Get that camera ready; you'll want to capture every flip, flop, and adorable stumble.

Now, onto the implications. Yes, I know we've already babyproofed, but now it becomes the next Olympic sport for you. And no, I don't mean putting a foam pad on that one coffee table corner. I mean the full-blown, farewell-to-your-stylish-living-room kind of babyproofing. Those beloved decorative items? They're about to take an extended vacation.

But let's not overlook the fun stuff. Those "I'm trying so hard" faces as they pull themselves across the room? Pure gold. And the mess—oh, the glorious chaos. You'll discover things you didn't even know you owned. It's like a magical treasure hunt, only without the treasure and more dust bunnies.

Ensuring Safety During This Phase

You thought changing diapers was a challenge? Try keeping up with a six-month-old gymnast! One second, they're lying there all innocent-like, and the next, BAM! They've gone full ninja, rolling, and crawling towards new horizons. But don't worry, this is all part of the show, and you're the lucky director. You'll cheer them on, capture those first flips on camera (always keep it handy), and marvel at the way they're discovering the world—one tiny, determined movement at a time.

And with mobility, babyproofing 2.0 becomes your primary sport. Say goodbye to breakables at baby's reach and hello to the thrilling game of "Find the Hazard." You'll be scouring corners for lurking danger like a seasoned detective. Also, brace for some surprising finds—lost keys, that other sock, maybe even your sanity. Your tiny treasure hunter will find everything you didn't know you'd lost. It's a whole new world.

Now, the real fun begins, Dad. You've got a mobile munchkin, and safety's the name of the game. Here's your game plan:

- **Crawl's Eye View**: Get down on all fours and scout the terrain from their perspective. If it looks tempting and dangerous, it's gotta go!
- **Baby-proofing Reboot**: It's time to fortify those defenses again. Check Chapter 1; trust me, it's worth revisiting.
- **Safe Spaces Assemble**: Set up a fortress of fun where they can roam free. Play mats, soft rugs, gates—make it a haven of exploration.
- **Embrace the Mayhem**: Yup, it's going to get messier, Dad. You're now the janitor of a one-baby circus. Invest in that oversized broom and make clean-up time a dad-baby bonding ritual!
- **Hawk Eye**: Keep those fatherly instincts sharp. Your baby's counting on you to spot those little dangers and capture those significant milestones.
- **The Comfort Zone**: There'll be tumbles, and you'll be there with a hug, a goofy face, or a gentle word. They'll bounce back faster with Dad by their side.

There it is new Dad: the sixth chapter of your thrilling adventure. You're not just observing; you're part of the action. Cherish it, capture it, and whatever you do, don't blink. This tiny explorer has a world to conquer; you're their guide! Welcome to the next level of parenting.

The First Crawl

Michael shared his story on the first crawl.

There I was, sprawled out on the floor next to my tiny partner-in-crime, surrounded by what looked like the aftermath of a toy store explosion. And I swear it sounded like gears grinding in my little one's noggin. It's the kind of plotting and planning you'd expect from a cartoon villain, but way cuter.

And then, as if on cue, I caught that mischievous twinkle in his eye. Out of nowhere - boom! The epic roll. I watched in awe as this mini-me pulled off a smooth transition from back to belly, like he was born for it.

But plot twist! Just when I thought that roll had stolen the show, a few curtain calls later, he decided it was time for the crawling sequel. Visualize it like the climax of an action-packed movie - my little guy, positioning his teeny hands with determination, mentally piecing together the whole "forward movement" concept. And bam! He nailed it.

Sure, it started as more of a "commando-drag" than a classic crawl, but who's nitpicking? Seeing that fierce determination in my pocket-sized explorer as he inched closer to his toy was priceless. And that smug look he gave me afterward? It was as if he was saying, "You seeing this, Dad? I'm about two steps away from taking over the household!"

SECTION 2: INTRODUCTION TO SOLIDS

Alright, dad, grab your bib—it's not just baby who'll need it. We're about to dive into the chaotic world of infant gastronomy, where puréed avocados are the new caviar, and every meal is a potential viral video in the making. It's the six-month milestone, and your baby's about to go culinary exploring. Get ready for flavor town, baby, and your adorable, soon-to-be-messy kiddo.

When and How to Introduce Solids to Baby

The Timeline: Six months might be the typical starting line, but babies are like snowflakes—no two are alike. Keep an eye out for the "I'm ready for more than just milk, Dad!" signals:

- They can sit up without flopping over like a deflated balloon animal.
- They're eyeing your pizza slice with a look that says, "I'm coming for you next."
- Their tongue's not playing goalie anymore, blocking all solid foods from entering the mouth-net.

The Culinary Adventure:

- **The First Steps**: Start with the baby's equivalent of fine dining—mashed bananas, puréed avocados, or baby-gourmet sweet potatoes. Introduce one food at a time—

it's like pacing episodes of a favorite show. You don't want to binge-watch the whole season in a day.

- **The Right Moment**: Timing's as crucial as it is when pulling off a witty one-liner. Happy baby = adventurous eater. Cranky baby = food critic.
- **The Consistency**: Think soupy first. You can dial back on the liquid as they become the Gordon Ramsay of the highchair.
- **The Baby's Pace**: You're not leading a marching band here. Let them explore, taste, and wear their food. They'll get the hang of it.
- **The Mess Factor**: Oh boy, things will get messy. Picture a food fight but cuter. Grab those photos; they're gold!
- **The Transition**: Slowly introduce finger foods, like soft cheese or ripe fruit. Think of them as baby tapas.
- **The Safety Net**: Keep an eye out, champ. No popcorn, whole nuts, or grapes. They're not quite ready for that level of snacking.
- **The Experience**: Enjoy every slurp, giggle, and yogurt facial. It's a time to remember. Bon appétit, baby!

Dealing With Picky Eaters

Picky eater on your hands? Fear not, here's the playbook:

- **Stay Cool**: Carrots got the cold shoulder? It's alright. It's like they're trying on different taste outfits.
- **Persistence Pays Off**: Keep introducing new foods. Persistence can turn "Eww" into "Yum!"

- **Creative Cooking**: Think of it as a culinary mash-up. Mix favorites with newbies.
- **Monkey See, Monkey Eat**: Eat your greens, and they might just follow suit.
- **No Bribes or Force**: This isn't a hostage negotiation. Keep it positive.
- **Tiny Portions**: It's tapas time, not Thanksgiving dinner.
- **Stay on Schedule**: Regular meal times keep hunger and readiness in sync.

There you have it: keep it fun, roll with the spills, and remember, you're crafting your little food critic's palate. Before you know it, they'll be asking for extra olives in their puréed peas. Enjoy the culinary adventure! It's a delicious ride.

Messy Eater

There I was, ready to embark on this great adventure known as "feeding my baby something other than milk." The plan was simple: mashed bananas. Easy, right? I mean, how hard could it be? Bananas are the friendly fruit, the smooth jazz of the food world.

I had everything laid out, spoon poised, looking into those big, innocent eyes that had no idea the culinary delight that was about to happen. And then, in what can only be described as a spectacular mishap worthy of a slow-motion replay, those tiny little hands shot up and grabbed the spoon. Bananas everywhere. In the hair, on the cheeks, probably even in places I didn't discover until much later.

I'd love to tell you that I handled it with grace and poise, but no, I was caught in this bewildered state between "What just happened?" and "Is this really my life now?" But then, that laughter. Oh boy, that baby giggle that can melt even the most banana-covered heart. My tiny little artist was painting a masterpiece with mashed bananas, and I was the lucky audience.

The kitchen was a mess, sure. But in that moment, all that mattered was this fantastic little person discovering joy in the simplest of things. I found myself laughing right along with them, both of us covered in bananas and kinda loving the moment.

It's funny how the messiest, most unexpected situations often turn into the best memories. It was supposed to be a simple meal. It turned into an unforgettable experience. And you know what? I wouldn't trade it for the world. Even if it did take forever to clean up the banana battleground.

SECTION 3: TEETHING TROUBLES

Teething that magical time when your little one's first chompers decide to make their debut, transforming your usually happy-go-lucky bundle of joy into a drooling, chewing, occasionally cranky phenomenon. Here's what you need to know:

Recognizing Signs of Teething and Ways to Soothe the Pain

If you suddenly find yourself in a puddle of drool or notice that your baby is gnawing on everything in sight (including your prized possessions), congratulations, you've got a teether! Here's a handy field guide:

Signs of Teething

- **Drool City**: Enough drool to fill a kiddie pool? That's teething for you.
- **Chew-Mania**: Everything's fair game. Toys, fingers, the family pet. No judgments here.
- **Irritability**: Think less 'angelic baby' and more 'cranky rockstar.'
- **Gum Alert**: Red, sore, swollen gums? The teeth are coming.
- **Sleep Strike**: Some nights, sleep becomes a distant memory.

Soothing Strategies

- **Teething Toys**: Silicone or rubber toys can be like a mini spa day for their gums.
- **Cold Comfort**: Chill (but don't freeze) a wet washcloth or teething ring. Instant relief.
- **Magic Touch**: Your finger + gentle gum massage = Happy baby.
- **Teething Gels**: Consult your baby's doc first, but these can be game changers.

Navigating Baby's Mood Swings During This Phase

Teething can bring out a rollercoaster of emotions in your baby, and it's completely normal. Teething can feel like a baby's first mid-life crisis. Here's how to keep things cool:

- **Stay Chill**: They're uncomfortable, not possessed. Deep breaths. You've got this.
- **Cuddle Power**: Sometimes, extra hugs are the best medicine.
- **Distraction Tactic**: A fun game or silly dance can be the spoonful of sugar needed.
- **Flexible Feeding**: If they turn down chow time, just roll with it.
- **Routine is Key**: Predictability can be a calming balm.
- **Super Dad Self-Care**: Hand off to a partner when you need a break. Recharging is essential.
- **Cuddle Fest**: More cuddles? Yes, please. It's a bonding extravaganza.
- **Keep the Faith**: This too shall pass. Soon, you'll have your smiley munchkin back.

Embrace the chaos, the mess, and even the tears (yours and theirs). After all, one day, these teeth will be demanding a visit from the Tooth Fairy, and you'll look back and laugh. In the meantime, cherish the ups, the downs, and everything in between. You're doing an extraordinary job in this grand adventure known as "dadhood."

FATHERHOOD QUEST – ULTIMATE TUMMY TIME

Level 1: The Newbie Challenge

Stretch out that tummy time for a few extra seconds daily. Simple, right? If you're cheering after a minute, don't worry, that's perfectly normal. Feeling like a champ for that one-minute victory is your achievement here. It's like winning gold but without the national anthem playing.

Level 2: Getting Down and Personal

It's time to get down on the floor. You're now part of this tummy spectacle, and you need to make it count. Your achievement is your shared giggles and the realization that you both look equally silly. Embrace it; it's the good stuff.

Level 3: The Toy Tease

Place their favorite toys just out of reach. It's not cruel; it's motivation! Baby's first reach, grab, and conquer is your achievement. They're now ready for world domination, one toy at a time.

Level 4: Playful Interaction

Who says tummy time must be all business? Make funny faces, poke out your tongue, and engage in peek-a-boo fun. Watch as your baby reacts, mimics, and perhaps even initiates a play. The achievement here is laughter, connection, and maybe the discovery that you've got the makings of a comedian—or at least someone who can make a six-month-old giggle. Now, that's memorable.

Think of this quest as less as baby gymnastics and more as a bonding session with a sprinkle of insanity. If parenting were a game, this would be the fun level. Let's break it down:

Oh, and just a heads-up, next up in Chapter 7, we've got baby babbling. Ready to decode your tiny human's first attempts at communication? It's like deciphering ancient runes but cuter. Get ready to embrace the delightful chaos of baby talk!

7

MONTH NINE—THE ART OF BABBLING AND CLAPPING

H oly crap, you've made it to month nine! First off, virtual high five! Your kid is about to enter the elite club of baby chit-chat; exciting, right? Now, put on your interpreter's hat because you're about to become fluent in baby-talk.

SECTION 1: UNDERSTANDING BABY TALK

At nine months old, your baby's babbling is more than just sweet sounds—it's their way of experimenting with sounds, mimicking your speech, and trying to communicate with you. You'll be amazed as they string together consonants and vowels, creating their own unique language.

Recognizing the Stages of Baby Talk and Its Significance

That's not just random noise. Your little one is a budding conversationalist, testing out new sounds and creating a symphony of high-end consonants and vowels. It's like jazz but cuter. From melodious goo-goos to rhythmic ga-gas, your child's becoming a linguistic wizard. It's more than just gibberish; it's the building blocks of language itself! Your baby's turning into a tiny talk show host, ready to engage you in some serious chat. And while you might not catch every word, just go with the flow—embrace the confusion, respond to their sounds, and enjoy the comedy gold that ensues.

But do not worry if you can't decipher every syllable. Baby talk is a quirky language all on its own, and it's filled with hilarious distortions. Embrace the giggles, respond to their babbling, and watch their language journey unfold.

Encouraging Language Development Through Interaction

Get set because you've just been handed the most crucial role of your life, and it's starring as the host, comedian, actor, and #1 fan of the tiniest, cutest audience on the planet.

Now picture this: You're standing in your kitchen, whipping up breakfast. Except now, it's not just eggs and bacon; it's "Breakfast with Dad," the hottest new show on the food network. The audience of one is hooked, and every flip of the pancake is a five-star event!

Your baby's watching, why not turn diaper-changing into a stand-up routine? "Hey, kiddo, ever wonder why diapers are like politicians? They both need changing regularly—for the same reason!" Cue adorable giggles and snorts.

And then there's story time. Forget the monotone reading; you're directing a one-person Broadway show. Each character has a voice, every page turn is a plot twist, and those little wide eyes are your rave reviews.

But the encore? That's when they babble back, and it sounds like they've just delivered the speech of a lifetime. "Wow, that's some profound wisdom you've got there, buddy!" you'll say, clapping like they've just solved world peace.

Welcome to the whirlwind world of parenting, where every day's a performance, and your baby's the critic, the fan, and the co-star. Enjoy the spotlight!

Justin's Baby

Let me tell you about my buddy, Justin. This guy? He's turned the art of parenting into an Oscar-worthy performance. Forget basic bedtime stories; in Justin's house, the living room's a full-blown theater where tales come to life. And when it's splash time? Those rubber ducks aren't just floating; they're giving dramatic monologues in the tub.

And here's the kicker: Justin's other half is fluent in Spanish. So, their kiddo? He's getting a double dose of linguistic magic. It's not just about vocab drills for them; it's crafting those memories, cherishing the chuckles, and mixing the mundane with a little sprinkle of "mágico." For Justin, this isn't just a parenting gig; it's embracing the weird, wondrous journey of dadhood.

SECTION 2: APPRECIATING THE SMALL WINS

Parenting is a roller coaster, but not the terrifying kind. It's more like the one where you laugh your head off as you wobble around. You'll have your ups, downs, and some sticky moments (both emotionally and literally, thanks to spilled juices).

But here's the best part: It's those seemingly mundane moments that stand out. The real wins are the joy when they first mimic a sound or that proud moment when they start clapping, realizing they've done something amazing.

Keep enjoying these moments. You're doing a fabulous job navigating the fascinating world of baby linguistics. Keep those conversations going, and soon enough, you'll have a tiny chatterbox ruling the roost.

Recognizing and Celebrating Baby's Small Milestones

Parenting's kinda like being the spectator at the world's tiniest, most endearing Olympics. Every little thing they do? Yeah, that's them winning a gold medal in our hearts. Like when they flash that gummy grin or offer up a coo – that's your kiddo saying, "Hey, I'm getting this social thing."

Then there's the grand performance of the roll. From back to belly and back again, it's like witnessing a pint-sized acrobat in action. And when they sit up all by themselves? That's them taking the throne, ready to rule their tiny kingdom.

Moving right to the baby crawling marathon – it's equal parts adorable and "Oh man, I should've baby-proofed sooner." (Which you've done right?). Watching them bravely tackle the living room floor is like watching a mini explorer discover new lands.

And let's talk about those shaky, bambi-leg moments. As they stand and attempt those first unsure steps, it's like watching a tiny gladiator enter the arena. By the way, brace yourself for their first words. It might be a "mama, " a "dada," or their favorite, uninterpretable babble. Whatever it is, it's pure platinum. Go ahead and grab your front-row seat because these little moments? They're the main event.

How to Stimulate and Support These Milestones

Great, you want to be the Spielberg of your baby's developmental years? Well, it's been a unpredictable adventure so far.

- **Create a Wonderland**: Think of toys, books, and sensory objects like the props in a big-budget film. Make it colorful, make it exciting, and watch their tiny eyes light up. Who knew a squeaky duck could be such a scene-stealer?
- **Interactive Play Time**: This is where you get down and dirty with some serious baby-talk improv. Peek-a-boo, silly songs, babble mimicry - it's a two-person comedy routine, and your co-star drools. It's a hit show every time.
- **Tummy Time Trials**: Picture this as the baby's personal training montage. It's like "Rocky," but with more adorable flailing. Builds muscles and sets up future crawling stardom. Make sure to cue the inspirational music.
- **Cheerleading Squad of One**: Every milestone? It's your cue to go full Broadway audience. The sitting, the

standing, those wobbly first steps? All deserve a
standing ovation. They're your little star, after all.

- **Adventure Playground**: Babyproofing isn't just about
safety; it's about building a stage where they can
perform. Create a space that screams, "Go ahead,
explore; I've covered the sharp corners." They'll thank
you with a victorious baby giggle.
- **The Secret Sauce – Love and Cuddles**: When the lights
dim and the toys are put away, it's the snuggles and
gentle whispers that make them feel like they can take
on the world - or at least the living room. Now, bring
on the love. It's the encore they'll always want.

Parenting's a production, and you're the director, producer, and
number one fan. Enjoy the show.

Matt and Baby Izzy

*There I was, one bright and sunny morning, watching my girl Izzy
squirm about during her tummy time. And guess what? She went and
lifted her little head up for the first time. It was a significant milestone, and both Jennifer and I made a huge fuss over her.*

*Izzy's giggles and babbles kept us laughing and engaging, and I swear
Jennifer and I knew more about each other's days because of the way
we were engaging with Izzy. One evening, I was just messing around,
pulling out some crazy dance moves (dance parties became our thing),
and what does she do? She claps her little hands together. That set us
all off, me and her mom included, clapping along.*

*The milestones kept coming. One afternoon, she just decided she had
enough of crawling and took her first wobbly steps. I couldn't help but*

be amazed, and I managed to pull out the phone in time to take a short video. I may have accidentally sent it to my group chat at work, but thankfully, they were as thrilled as we were. Those wins, as tiny as they might be, were some real golden moments for us.

SECTION 3: BALANCING WORK AND BABY

Juggling the demands of work while embracing fatherhood? Trust me, you're not alone in this circus. It's a challenge most dads grapple with, especially when your career's at a pivotal juncture, beckoning you to scale new heights. But hey, those first giggles, steps, and school plays—they're beckoning too. The goal? Discovering balance that resonates with you and your tribe.

Navigating the Challenges of Balancing Work and Fatherhood

Being a working dad and not losing your marbles is a tightrope walk. Here's a couple pointers that worked for us:

- **The Conversation Tango**: Talking your way through tricky waters? A strength. Craft that duo dance with your partner, discussing rhythms and routines. It's a two-step process filled with give and take.
- **Matrix Moves**: Visualize an overwhelming tide of tasks. Now imagine ducking and dodging with flair. Prioritize, pivot, and occasionally—just let go.
- **Digital Hugs**: Pining for your munchkin? Queue up that video call. Consider it your daily dose of sunshine on a cloudy workday.

- **Presence Waltz**: Here's the trick: Be wholly present. Whether it's marveling at mashed pea artistry or their attempt at a first word—savor these golden snippets.
- **Recharge Routine**: Drained? Refuel. Whether it's breaking a sweat or simply sipping that perfectly brewed coffee. Refreshed dad vibes translate to a chirpier household.
- **Backup Beat**: Loop in your support crew. Think of them as the co-stars in your fatherhood saga. A cameo by grandma or a sitter can be a game-changer.

And Hey, Celebrate! The wins, the almost-wins, even the losses. Savor the chaos, laugh at the mistakes, and high-five yourself every once in a while. Because trust me, seeing your little one grow and thrive? That's the real paycheck.

Darmian and Work Commitments

As a first-time dad, juggling work and commitments with my baby's routines was both exciting and challenging. Open communication with my employer about my new responsibilities as a father was crucial, and I was fortunate to have their support in adjusting my schedule occasionally.

Despite the unpredictability of my baby's sleep schedule, I stayed focused and productive at work by organizing tasks efficiently and even stealing power naps during lunch breaks. My partner and I worked as a team, establishing a consistent schedule for our baby's needs, which strengthened our bond as parents.

Flexibility was key, allowing me to be present for my family while fulfilling my work responsibilities. It was a balancing act that brought immense joy and fulfillment as I embraced this new chapter of my life.

FATHERHOOD QUEST: SOUND MAESTRO

Level 1: Babble Boss Battle:

Baby talk is in the air! Engage in this delightful duel of sounds. Respond to those coos as if they're the keys to a treasure trove. Here's where the quest commences, noble adventurer.

Level 2: Dynamic Duo Debut:

Flex those singing muscles. It's a symphonic showdown—with your mini-me in tow. Whether it's 'Old MacDonald' or 'Baa Baa Black Sheep,' be ready for some unexpected solos or, more likely, drool.

Level 3: Rhythm Ranger Rumble:

Got beats? Flaunt them. It's time for a musical rally, be it clapping, snapping, or a belly drum bonanza. And hey, a custom jingle for diaper time? Legendary!

Level 4: Maestro's Magnum Opus:

The crescendo! Embark on an auditory adventure, exploring every chuckle, jingle, and, yes, those endearing baby toots. Watch in wonder as their sound skills ascend to a magnum opus. Take a bow, Maestro! You've orchestrated a masterpiece.

As we segue into Chapter 8, ponder upon William Wordsworth's wisdom: "The child is the father of the man." (Khurana, 2019). With each tick of the clock, our little ones unfurl, with every moment etching an indelible mark on their destinies. Here's to celebrating these marvels hand in hand.

.

8

MONTH 12—THE BIG ONE

H old onto your hats, gents! The grand finale of your first year on this whirlwind parenting rollercoaster is fast approaching. And the main event? Your tiny tot's heroic attempt to stand tall on two wobbly legs.

This isn't merely a milestone; it's their opening act in a long series of adventures. Ready your cameras and perhaps some protective bubble wrap because this chapter is more than just about their growth. It's the thrilling chapter titled: "I blinked, and now where's the baby?"

SECTION 1: PREPARING FOR THE FIRST BIRTHDAY

Brace yourself because you and your partner are about to mastermind your baby's first birthday bash. Think of yourselves as the Spielberg and Lucas of party planning. Magic meets the mayhem.

Planning a Meaningful and Memorable First Birthday

Choosing the perfect theme is a quest you'll embark on together. Whether it's fairy princesses in space or a safari in your backyard, the sparks of your combined creativity will light up the room. Those decorations? Think of them as more than just eye candy; they're a canvas showcasing your collective love and personality.

And that cake smash? It's the scene-stealing climax. As your kiddo plunges face-first into the frosting, that shared glance between you two screams, "Yup, all the caffeine-fueled nights were worth it." Make sure to snap that moment. It's Oscar-worthy.

From invites to icing, each detail is a poignant dance between you and your co-director. You're not merely throwing a party; you're crafting a debut movie. Toast with your apple juices; here's to the best premiere ever!

When considering the guest list, aim for cozy over chaotic. A smaller circle means fewer overwhelmed baby tears. And, bonus, more cake for you.

Lastly, don't get lost in the sequins and sparkle. The essence lies in celebrating the epic saga of year one and the delight your baby has brought into your life. Revel in every giggle, toothless grin, and heartwarming mess. It's the opening sequence of a lifetime of blockbusters with your mini-leading star.

How to Manage the Chaos of a Baby Party

Unraveling the pandemonium of a baby party requires a solid checklist, milk bottles on standby, and a mountain of wipes. Keep it breezy, and when in doubt, remember there's no shame in summoning backup. And remember, a sleepy baby is a grumpy baby.

SECTION 2: BABY'S FIRST STEPS

Your pint-sized human's now in the "furniture surfing" phase, clinging onto anything resembling stability. That includes your clueless fingers. Embrace your new job title: Official Human Walker.

Understanding the Significance of Baby's First Steps

Those wobbly steps aren't just an adorable party trick. Imagine handing your child the passport to an undiscovered world filled with mysterious crevices (mostly hiding crumbs). It's a lesson in physics, spatial awareness, and the good ol' push and pull-effect. These first steps are the tickets to an enhanced cognitive ride. And emotionally? That pride in their eyes when they nail it? Think of it as them clinching gold in the Toddler Olympics.

How to Support and Encourage Your Baby During This Phase

Your tiny Neil Armstrong's about to take their giant leap into your shaggy carpet, and you're ground control.

- **Safety First**: Toddler-proof everything. Pointy? Hide it. Wobbly? Toss it.

- **Lend a Hand**: Literally. It's like stabilizers for those teeny shoes.
- **Cheer On**: Be their biggest fan. Your cheer can make them feel like they're walking on the moon.
- **Celebrate**: Every step is an event. Think confetti, air horns, and the whole shebang.
- **Patience, Padawan**: They'll find their footing. Just breathe.
- **Temptation Tactics**: Introduce standing-friendly toys. It's a carrot on a stick, but 1000 times more adorable.

Suit up, Coach. This is your field day.

Anthony and Vanessa

Here is Anthony's amazing story of his experience when he witnessed his girl take her first steps.

I was sitting on the living room floor with my one-year-old daughter, Vanessa, who was happily playing with her toys. She had been standing and cruising along the furniture for a while, but she hadn't taken any independent steps yet. As I scrolled through my phone, I heard a sudden commotion coming from the other side of the room.

I looked up just in time to see Vanessa let go of the coffee table and take her very first wobbly step toward me. My heart skipped a beat, and I couldn't believe what I was witnessing! There she was, my little princess, taking those brave steps all on her own.

Exhilaration and panic washed over me simultaneously. I couldn't contain my excitement and shouted, "Vanessa, you are walking! You did it!" But as she took a few more steps, my panic set in. I quickly realized that she was headed straight for the TV stand, which was not baby-proofed.

In a split second, I lunged forward, arms outstretched, and managed to scoop Vanessa up just in time before she could reach the TV stand. She looked up at me with a mixture of surprise and delight, seemingly proud of her accomplishment, while I was still catching my breath from the adrenaline rush.

From that moment on, it was a whirlwind of joy and constant vigilance. Vanessa was thrilled with her newfound ability to walk that she wanted to explore every corner of the house. I followed closely behind her, ready to catch her if she stumbled, and made sure that every nook and cranny was baby-proofed.

Watching Vanessa take her first steps was an unforgettable experience, filled with both amazement and the realization that my baby was growing up so fast.

SECTION 3: REFLECTING ON THE FIRST YEAR

Has it been a year already? It's mind-boggling. One minute, you're gingerly handling this newborn who's looking up at you with such trust, and in the blink of an eye, they're on the move, channeling their inner explorer—minus the gear.

With each burp and giggle, you swell with a mix of pride and disbelief. They grow up incredibly fast that it makes even the most rapid tech advancements seem laggy. And sure, your living room? Well, it's been commandeered by toys. But that's the mark of a home filled with adventure and memories. Welcome to the world of fatherhood, year one down.

The Growth of a Baby and a Dad—A Reflective Overview

One of my really good friends, Jamie, shared his overview of his baby's growth and the journey toward fatherhood. I hope you enjoy it.

My friend, let me share with you this incredible journey of becoming a dad that's been my life's adventure this past year. It's been full of discovery, joy, challenges, and the type of love that you can't quite put into words.

From that very first cuddle, life took a beautiful turn. Sleepless nights, endless diaper changes? They're nothing compared to the overwhelming connection and bond we've formed.

Witnessing her growth, those first wobbly steps and the spark in her eyes as she explores has been an absolute privilege. And the patience and resilience that comes with it? They've become my new best mates.

Those little babbles turning into "Dada"—it's pure magic. It's like having a secret chat that only the two of us understand.

I've also learned the importance of balance and self-care on this journey. Taking a moment for myself and asking for help from friends and family—it's been vital.

It's been a journey of growth, not just for her but for me as well. I've discovered new strengths and faced fears with courage I didn't know I had.

Looking ahead, the excitement continues. More challenges, more milestones, but with a beaming smile, I'm ready to face them all.

And here's the promise, the core of it all: being there for her, cheering her on, and being her biggest supporter. Fatherhood has given my life a deeper meaning, and I'm grateful every day.

Here's to growth, both for my little one and for me as a dad. Together, we're embracing this beautiful adventure, creating memories to cherish. I can't wait to see what's next for our family. Cheers!

Lessons Learned, Cherished Memories, and Challenges Overcome

As this first tumultuous ride of a year in the parenthood theme park comes to a close, we're pausing for a well-deserved "Did we really just do that?" moment. It's been like riding a rollercoaster blindfolded, but man, what a trip of love and leveling up.

Lessons from the Frontline:

- **The Patience Game**: Let's face it, between the sleepless serenades and epic diaper explosions, Zen-like patience isn't just helpful; it's survival gear.
- **The Art of Going with It**: Turns out babies never got the memo about our plans. Rolling with their whims? That's our new superpower.
- **Looking After Numero Uno**: Remember the oxygen mask rule on planes? Same logic. A bit of me-time, a chapter of a book, or just some deep, sanity-saving breaths—golden.

As we approach the end of this incredible first year of parenthood, we can't help but reflect on the many lessons we have learned, the cherished memories we've created, and the challenges we've overcome together. It's been a rollercoaster ride, but one filled with love and growth.

Memory Hall of Fame:

- **The Great Meltdown**: Not the diaper kind, mind you. That first smile from your little one? It's like a ray of sunshine armed with laser-guided precision aimed right at your heartstrings. Target acquired.
- **The Giggle Symphony**: Oh, those baby laughs. That sound could end wars, cure the common cold, and possibly even make your favorite sports team win. Pure, bottled joy.
- **Magic Milestone Markers**: Rolling over, the army crawl, those first wobbly steps - it's like watching a very determined, pint-sized explorer conquer the world one impressive feat at a time. Pure magic, only without the magician's hat.

Challenges Overcome

Here's the highlight reel of challenges conquered, and yes, it comes with badges:

- **The Night Owls' Club**: Those early months felt like an extended director's cut of an insomnia-fueled movie. But with teamwork and a bit of mutual delirium, you and your partner became a dynamic duo, battling the sleepless nights.

- **The Life Juggling Act**: Between work, family, and sneaking in those precious five minutes for yourself (hello, bathroom break!), achieving balance was like nailing a trapeze act. But hey, priorities became more apparent, and somehow, you found a way to make the moments count.
- **Decision-making Decathlon**: Parenting choices had you feeling like a contestant on a high-stakes game show? No worries. You went with your gut, talked it out, and picked Door Number 'Whatever Works Best for Baby.'

Through the rollercoaster of highs, lows, and those weird in-between moments, you discover that parenthood isn't a fixed recipe. It's more of a "taste-as-you-go" cooking adventure. Each day serves up fresh lessons, unforgettable memories, and a big slice of humble pie. Feel free to take a victory lap. You've earned it.

Documenting Your Journey

- **A Time Capsule with Tiny Footprints**: Jotting down those memories isn't just a sentimental journey through baby's greatest hits like first smiles, infectious babbles, or those wobbly attempts at walking. It's a way to freeze time, creating a scrapbook you both can leaf through in those teenage rebellion years (brace yourself!).

- **Dad 2.0 - Reflections on the Journey**: This isn't just about tracking spit-up stats. Writing about the uncontrolled ride of fatherhood helps you see what worked (that lullaby) and what didn't (that other lullaby). It's a highlight reel of triumphs and those "learning experiences" that shape the fine art of parenting.
- **A Legacy in Ink**: These reflections aren't just for you; they're a hand-me-down of memories for your kid. One day, they'll flip through your words and see the world as you did when they were tiny, exploring every cuddle, every milestone, and probably laughing at your sleep-deprived typos.

In the end, it's more than a journal; it's a heartfelt conversation with the future. It's leaving a trace of love, joy, and those everyday dad-hero moments for the next generation.

FATHERHOOD QUEST: JOURNEY THROUGH YEAR ONE

It was a significant chapter, therefore, it's a big quest. Let's embark on a three-level adventure that's as rewarding as accidentally finding that lost pacifier at 3 a.m.

Level 1: The First Birthday Bonanza

Theme It Up: Based on your baby's current obsession (even if it's the ceiling fan), theme the day. Make it about them.

Snack Attack: Whip up some baby-friendly treats. Think soft, squishy, and hopefully not all over the carpet.

Memory Lane: Create a photo timeline from day one to now. Be prepared for waterworks — mostly yours.

Level 2: The Wobbly Walkabout

Safari Zone: Make your living space a 'discovery zone.' Soft corners, exciting textures, and the odd squeaky toy.

Cheer Squad: Every tiny step deserves a standing ovation. Yes, you're now the pep squad. Embrace it.

Walk the Talk: Help them cruise using furniture, toys, or, let's face it, the family pet.

Level 3: Memory Capsule Craze

Dear future Them: Write a letter to your child to open on their 18th birthday.

Babbles to Words: Document the cute mispronunciations. Trust me, they're comedy gold.

Highlight Reel: Film or snap photos of everyday moments because today's normal is tomorrow's nostalgic tear-jerker.

Here's to making every level count!

9

EMBRACING TODDLERHOOD

W elcome to negotiating with your toddler, the tiniest, most stubborn diplomat you'll ever meet. Get ready for both tantrums and heart-melting first words. Leveling up in the parenting game, are we? Prepare yourself for a parenting experience that's a unique blend of mayhem and magic.

SECTION 1: THE TODDLER TRANSITION

Your wee one is making the big jump from baby to toddler. It's the equivalent of trading in a scooter for a motorcycle—much faster, way more adventurous, and yes, accidents will happen.

What to Expect When Your Baby Becomes a Toddler

- **Wobbly Walks**: The first steps. It's less like a runway model's strut and more like a tipsy penguin. Every lunge forward, every unexpected face-plant, it's all part of the journey. And trust me, you'll be capturing every moment, even the ones they'd probably want erased from the family album later.

- **Utensil Underestimation**: Let's chat about spoons for a second. In their eyes, it's not just a spoon; it's a shiny, magical, multi-purpose tool. Eating? Sure. Drumming on the table? Absolutely. Pretending it's a plane? You bet. And sometimes, it's just about flinging mashed peas. Simple pleasures.

- **First Words, Sort Of**: As they begin to find their voice, expect a mix of profound gibberish. "Ba-ba" could mean "I'm hungry," "look at that bird," or perhaps, "I'm considering a career in quantum physics." It's a delightful guessing game. And every so often, they nail a word, and it's like they've just delivered the punchline to the world's best joke.

- **Moods That Shift Like Weather**: The emotions of a toddler are like living in a city that experiences all four seasons in a day. Sunshine giggles can cloud over in an instant, leading to a downpour of tears. But you? You're the trusty weatherman, always on hand with a comforting forecast and a cuddle umbrella.

Navigating Tantrums and Fostering Independence

The thing is toddlerhood is a lot like trying to solve a Rubik's Cube while riding a unicycle... on ice. It's fun, unpredictable, and occasionally messy.

When the toddler tempests roll in, remember they're just flexing their emotional muscles. A bit of drama? It's just part of the show. Think of yourself as their personal, highly underrated director, helping guide them through their scene. Keep your cool and offer a hug or an understanding nod. Sometimes, they just want to know they've got a captive audience.

Next stop, Independence Avenue. That "I got this!" attitude? Brace yourself because it's about to get a lot of play. Sure, it might result in socks on their hands and a yogurt hair mask but let them revel in their newfound autonomy. Celebrate their achievements, no matter how small, as it boosts their confidence.

Let them take the wheel occasionally. Whether they're assembling a wardrobe that defies all fashion logic or championing cookies as a breakfast food, give them some agency. Keep it in the safe zone, of course, by offering them options you can get behind.

Remember, navigating tantrums and fostering independence is not about perfect parenting; it's about learning and growing together, and remember to keep your camera handy. Because this? This is the stuff memories are made of.

Kevin and Gaby

Here is Kevin sharing a small story about how he used innovative strategies to handle Gaby's independence.

Let me paint a picture for you: Gaby, in full superhero gear, ready to hit the park. Now, I could've said no, but instead, I decided, "Every superhero needs a sidekick!" There we were Batman and Robin, owning that playground, saving the day from imaginary villains. And when it was time to leave? That's when the real fun started: a chase all the way home, giggling like two kids.

Bath time at my house? It's a bubble adventure. Rubber duckies on missions across an ocean of bubbles. And bedtime? That's a quest, folks. We're searching for magical dreams under those cozy blankets, turning the ordinary into something extraordinary.

What's the lesson here? You've got to think outside the box. You've got to get down on their level and make the every day special. Because that's what being a parent is all about making memories, having fun, and turning the mundane into pure magic.

SECTION 2: EARLY EDUCATION AND PLAY

Imagine your toddler's mind as a blank canvas, eagerly waiting for the first strokes of color and imagination. Just like a budding artist, their early education and stimulation play a vital role in shaping the masterpiece of their future.

Understanding the Importance of Early Education and Stimulation

Think of early education for your toddler as the hidden level in a video game. Once you unlock it, you're on a path filled with curiosity, creativity, and maybe a few booby traps, but hey, that's parenting. It's not just about ABCs and 123s; it's about letting their imagination take flight, even if it means turning the living room into a jungle.

Interactive play? Reading together? Exploring the world? Yep, that's your new daily grind. And you'll love it. You'll be fueling their little minds, sparking their interest in learning, and probably learning a thing or two yourself, like the scientific reason why mud pies are gourmet food in the world of toddlers.

I suggest putting on your explorer's hat and embrace this stage with all its messy glory. You're not just their parent; you're their first teacher, guide, and partner in crime on this extraordinary quest. It's a journey that's going to shape both of you, you might as well hang on, dive in, and let the adventure begin. Trust me; there's no other ride quite like it.

Fun and Educational Play Ideas

As they continue to explore the world around them, these play ideas will spark their imagination and boost their early learning. In this adventurous chapter of parenting, the best learning happens through play, fun, and just a sprinkle of chaos.

- **Sensory Play Sensation**: Picture a sandbox, but replace the sand with colorful rice, water beads, or cloud dough. Let your kiddo dive in hands first. It's like an art installation that's meant to be destroyed – great for sensory development and imagination terrible for your vacuum cleaner.
- **Shape and Color Treasure Hunt**: Create your own living room Indiana Jones saga. Hide shapes and colors around the house and go on a quest to find them. Their mission: identify each find like a tiny art critic on a caffeine high. It's cognitive skills development with a side of adventure.

- **Storybook Theater**: Why read their favorite stories when you can perform them? Grab some funny hats, do voices that would make a cartoon character jealous, and act out a tale. It's Broadway on a budget, and they're both the star and the critic.

- **Alphabet Adventure**: Who needs a plain old scavenger hunt when you can go on an alphabet-themed one? Have them find objects corresponding to letters and let them lead the way. It's like an educational pirate map that doesn't lead to buried treasure but might lead to a buried remote control.

- **Kitchen Science Experiments**: Turn your kitchen into a low-budget, low-danger science lab. Think baking soda volcanoes and color-changing milk. They'll be fascinated, educated, and slightly messier than before. What's not to love?

Playtime

Introducing my tiny human to this uncharted territory of early education via play felt a bit like prepping for a heist - only with more snacks and fewer getaway cars. I aimed to turn learning into something that felt less like a chore and more like a scene from her favorite show.

Our top hit? Storybook theater. Picture this: a pile of vivid storybooks and the two of us gearing up for an imaginative journey. As I switched between voices that might make any cartoon character consider early retirement, her giggles became the day's soundtrack.

But where the real magic happened was our kitchen – suddenly transformed into a low-budget wizard's lab. Who knew that a simple baking soda and vinegar combo could rival a fireworks display? Or that swirling colors in milk could make both of us gawk like we'd just witnessed a minor miracle? Science: 1, Mundanity: 0.

SECTION 3: BUILDING A ROUTINE

Navigating the toddler years is a bit like piloting a spaceship through an asteroid field but with more drool and unpredictable explosions. That's where a consistent routine steps in like a trusty co-pilot. Imagine setting up daily waypoints like wake-up calls, meals, playtime escapades, those ever-elusive naptimes, and the grand finale of bedtime.

Sticking to this flight plan isn't just about clock-watching; it's about charting a course that meets your little astronaut's needs while sidestepping unnecessary turbulence (read: stress) for both Captain and crew. It's like giving them their own command center, where they can figure out the lay of the land, develop their own independence, and know what's coming up next on the journey. Just remember to pack extra snacks. Always pack extra snacks.

The Importance of a Consistent Routine for Toddlers

Toddlers and routine go together like peanut butter and jelly. It's about creating a rhythm to the day that's reassuring for them and, quite honestly, a bit of a lifesaver for you. (Lifehack: you may even be able to drink a warm cup of coffee.)

Starting the day off, right through meals, playtime, and the grand adventure to bedtime, having a routine builds a sense of familiarity. Think of it as giving your little one a preview of the day's script, helping them know their lines and cues. It's less about scheduling every minute and more about creating a comforting pattern that helps them understand what comes next.

And let's not forget the backstage benefits for you. A routine isn't just a toddler thing; it's your backstage pass to a more harmonious day. Knowing when those little breaks are coming, when it's time for a meal, and when you might get a moment to yourself? That's not just parenting; that's smart strategizing.

But hey, life's unpredictable, especially with a toddler running the show. Keep the routine, but don't be afraid to let it flex. Your little one will appreciate knowing what's coming up, but they'll also learn to roll with life's little surprises – just like you.

Tips for Setting a Practical Routine

Crafting a routine for your toddler isn't about creating the perfect script; it's about setting up a flow that works for both of you. Here's how to make it a hit:

- Maintain a consistent rhythm for meals, naps, and the all-important bedtime. Trust me, it's like magic for their sense of security (and your peace of mind).
- Stay tuned to your toddler's cues. Their patterns of hunger or tiredness? They're not just random; they're signals to shape the day.

- About bedtime? Craft a chill-out time that preludes it. A good sleep isn't just about recharging – it's the secret sauce for a more agreeable toddler.
- Yeah, a routine's golden, but flexibility's its best friend. When life throws a curveball, be ready to catch and adjust.
- Little Choices: Hand them the reins sometimes. Giving them a say makes them a partner in this adventure, not just a passenger.
- Keep It Simple: Your routine should be a gentle guide, not a military drill. Ease them into it.
- The Visual Aids: A chart or schedule they can see? That's like a treasure map for a toddler.
- Learn & Play: Insert fun learning stops along the way. It's like a mental jungle gym.

Patience, Grasshopper: Building a routine is like assembling LEGO without the instructions. It takes time to find the perfect fit, but once you do, it's worth the effort.

Sample Routine

Here's a sample daily routine for a toddler; we're talking about weekends here unless you're the primary parent.

Morning

- Wake up and have a cuddle session with dad or mom
- Breakfast together as a family
- Playtime with toys and books

Late Morning

- Snack time
- Outdoor play or a walk to the park
- Interactive learning activities, like sorting shapes or counting objects

Lunchtime

- Lunch with the family
- Quiet play, such as coloring or building blocks

Afternoon

- Nap time or rest time
- Snack and hydration

Late Afternoon

- Creative play, like drawing or imaginative play with toys
- Sensory activity, like playing with playdough or finger painting

Evening

- Dinner with the family
- Bath time and bedtime routine, including brushing teeth and reading a bedtime story
- Tuck-in and goodnight kisses

Remember, every child is different, and their routines may vary based on their individual needs and preferences. It's essential to tailor the routine to suit your toddler's temperament and developmental stage. Consistency and flexibility are crucial to creating a successful and enjoyable routine for both you and your little one.

FATHERHOOD QUEST: TANTRUM TAMER

Level 1: Breathe and stay calm

Take deep breaths and maintain your composure during the tantrum.

Level 2: Offer comfort

Gently hold your toddler and offer reassurance while using a soothing tone.

Level 3: Distract and redirect

Divert their attention to a favorite toy or activity to shift focus away from the tantrum.

Level 4: Validate feelings

Acknowledge their emotions and help them express their feelings in words.

CONCLUSION: LEVELING UP— THE GAME CONTINUES

Well, Dad, you've mastered the tutorial level, nailing the fine arts of diaper wizardry and insomnia. But hold those cheers; this is only the beginning. Ready for a sequel with greater challenges and even richer rewards?

It's hard to believe a year has zoomed past by since you started this incredible dad-venture? Let's hit pause for a sec and reminisce about our shared shenanigans.

From the nocturnal cries and diaper duels to the first unscripted grin and the heart-melting babble, you've been on a joyride with some sharp turns. Sure, it wasn't always smooth sailing, but you navigated the storm like a seasoned captain.

First steps? Check. The proud echoes of "Dada"? Oh yeah. You've donned the capes, delivered the laughs, and become the superstar in their universe.

This fatherhood role has been a greater teacher than any guide-book, turning you into a maestro of dad humor and the trust-your-gut kind of parent. The rulebook? Continuously rewritten, but that's where the fun lies.

Your kid's journey has twists and turns unique to the two of you. Every chapter with your little one is a personalized narrative. No two stories are the same. It's a dance, and you're both finding your rhythm.

Sure, you'll have those superhero moments and days when the cape's MIA. But here's the scoop: You're rocking this. Your love and steadfastness? They're the treasure.

Keep that heart open, that mind keen. Be flexible, learn, and savor. Even the stumbling blocks are part of this remarkable tale of Dadhood. Your love is their compass, guiding them through life's escapades. That's where the real victory is.

You've surfed the waves of babyhood with wisdom and passion. Now it's time to roll into the next exciting chapter, and guess what? More adventures await.

Go on, extraordinary Dad. Keep loving, laughing, and being the irreplaceable you. Relish each tick of the clock, each achievement, and keep that growing, learning, fun-loving bond with your kiddo.

Your heart is your Swiss Army knife in this fatherhood expedition. Let it guide you amidst the thrills and tests ahead.

Now, jump into the next phase with gusto and zeal. Dive into the wonders of toddlerhood and what's to come. Know that you're not just any dad; you're their dad, making a deep, indelible mark in a little life.

And hey, don't forget to enjoy the ride.

BONUS CHAPTER: TACKLING THE TRENCHES—COMMON STRUGGLES OF NEW DADS

Almost 10% of fresh-off-the-block dads face the daunting specter of paternal postnatal depression, an unwelcome guest few speak about (Cleveland Clinic, 2019). Fatherhood's got its spotlight moments but behind the curtain? We might be waging unseen wars. How about a flashlight for those darker corners.

SECTION 1: MANAGING WORK-LIFE BALANCE

Striving to be the perfect provider can weigh heavily on you. It's a noble goal, but not if it costs everything else. Taking care of yourself isn't a detour from responsibility; it's a part of it. Make the time to recharge, and never underestimate the importance of connecting with those closest to you. That balance isn't just healthy; it's essential. After all, what's the point of being the rock if you don't take a moment to enjoy the view with the people who count on you?

Navigating Paternity Leave and Returning to Work

Look, if you've got the shot at paternity leave, grab that chance. Honestly, it's a front-row seat to the early stages of dadhood — from the diaper duels to the sleepless symphonies that, for some weird reason, become heart-tugging moments you won't trade for anything.

Reality check: Resurfacing at work? Surreal. Yesterday, you were deep in lullabies; today? Drowning in emails. And yeah, sometimes Dave from Accounting's gibberish might remind you of baby talk.

Balancing the two worlds isn't a cakewalk. It's a delicate dance between boardrooms and baby rooms. But remember, you've got backup. Rely on your partner, find solace in fellow dad stories, or just find that one coffee shop guy who nails your order.

If you're knee-deep in paperwork but daydreaming of home, cut yourself some slack. It's not incompetence; it's just your priorities peeking through. Paternity leave is a brief blip, but the bond you're building with your kid? That's the stuff of legends.

Finding Balance Between Professional Commitments and Parenting

- Juggling work and a kiddo are the ultimate boss fight. Picture this: whipping up dinner, kid on the hip, phone buzzing non-stop. It's chaos, but it's your chaos.

- Bouncing between spreadsheets and pacifiers? You've got company. It's a whirlwind of midnight feeds and morning meetings.
- A couple of lifelines: Multitasking is your new superpower. Master the nap times; they're golden hours of productivity. And if things get too real? Call in reinforcements—friends, family, that teenager down the street who's saving for a bike.
- Virtual meetings? Oh, expect your toddler to crash them. But hey, they might just steal the show in a good way.

Relax occasionally. Life's not a leaderboard. It's about finding your rhythm, making memories, and sometimes just winging it. And by the looks of it, you're nailing this game.

Strategies to Advocate for Family-Friendly Policies at Work

Let's break this down and take a serious look at what you're aiming to achieve here. You're working on something vital - advocating for flexible work hours and parental leave policies. Let's get strategic, shall we?

- **Build Your Team**: Talk to your fellow dads, mom allies, and colleagues. This isn't about forming a superhero squad; it's about gathering like-minded people who understand the importance of what you're fighting for.
- **Craft Your Message**: Go ahead and put a smile on their faces with some dad humor. Humor is disarming and engaging. You're not just presenting an idea; you're connecting with your audience.

- **Display Confidence**: You're not just winging this; you've got facts and data. Let them see you as a parent and someone who understands the professional implications. Confidence comes from preparation, be ready.
- **Share Real Experiences**: You're not selling a product; you're advocating for something that matters to real people. Share what it's like the actual impact on daily life. Authenticity is compelling.
- **Negotiate Effectively**: You need to understand their perspective and what matters to them. Show them how these policies aren't just about goodwill; they make business sense. They benefit everyone.
- **Follow Up**: This isn't just a one-and-done deal. Stay engaged, offer updates, and provide success stories. Keep the conversation going.

You're likely to meet resistance. Keep in mind, though, that perseverance and endurance hold the secrets to success. It's not merely a negotiation; rather, it's a partnership. Time invested yields long term benefits, allowing relationships to flourish.

Instead of viewing "no" as finality, deem it "not yet". For advocates, patience resembles endurance during a prolonged race like a marathon, hoping success will soon be attained. At first, someone pitched an internal parental support initiative only to encounter rejection from higher-ups. Additional paternity leaves raised flags for worrying about absurd amounts of caretaker duties placed upon them by firms.

Yet, determined not to back down, After about nine months had passed since initially consulting them, they sent another questioning approach toward that business; ultimately answering answers with a fortified 'okay.' (ibid: Mihalich-Levin)

Make it happen. I believe you can.

SECTION 2: SUPPORTING YOUR PARTNER

Understanding Postpartum Depression and How to Support Your Partner Through It

Being a new dad is an odyssey of challenges, not just for you but for your partner as well. It's more than just the late-night feedings and never-ending diaper changes. Let's delve into an issue that's very real and affects countless families:

Postpartum depression touches about one in seven new moms. This isn't a trivial statistic (Cleveland Clinic, 2022). It's serious, and it might be unfolding in your own household. Here are a few suggestions on what to do:

- **Our Role as Dads**: It isn't about "fixing" things. This isn't a leaky faucet. It's about presence, understanding, and unwavering support.
- **Active Listening**: Truly listen without judgment. No dismissing their feelings. Offer an empathetic ear and a comforting shoulder.
- **Proactive Assistance**: Share household chores and baby care. Anticipate the needs without always being

asked. Think of it as a surprise encore in the concert of your daily life.

- **Educate Yourself**: Get to grips with what postpartum depression really signifies. It's neither a fleeting phase nor a sign of fragility. Consider delving into resources from organizations like the American Psychological Association or Postpartum Support International.
- **Encouragement**: Remind them of their strength and worth. Authentic recognition, especially recognizing their daily efforts, can be incredibly uplifting.
- **Seek Expert Assistance**: Don't wait for a crisis. Sometimes, professional intervention is crucial. Be willing to accompany them to appointments.
- **Champion Self-Care**: Propose to watch the baby, giving them an opportunity to rejuvenate. That pause might be transformational.
- **Patience is Key**: Healing takes time, much like brewing the perfect coffee. Both are worth the patience.

For more in-depth understanding, explore resources like the National Institute of Mental Health's insights on postpartum depression or engage with local support groups. Knowledge empowers, and empowerment is crucial.

Remember, we're not merely fathers but co-pilots in this journey. It's about teamwork, and as they say, teamwork is the dream's framework. Immerse yourself, be proactive, and embrace both the partner and father roles wholeheartedly. Together, we can weather this storm.

Keeping the Spark Alive: Ideas for Date Nights and Shared Experiences

I really want you to lean in here. Between diaper changes and the never-ending rendition of "Baby Shark," it's easy to put your relationship on the back burner. But hey, that love connection? It's not just the foundation of your family—it's the secret sauce. Let's look at ways to sprinkle a little extra seasoning on that:

- **In-house Ventures**: Cost-effective and intimate date nights can be as simple as trying out a new recipe or re-watching an old favorite movie. Consider an indoor picnic, creating a mini-festival ambiance just for two.
- **Starry-eyed Gatherings**: After bedtime stories, lounge under the stars in your backyard. It's an intimate space without the usual distractions.
- **Daylight Interactions**: Dates aren't only for nights. Enjoy a morning trek, a cycling escapade, or explore a nearby town. It's daytime romance at its best.
- **Creative Collaborations**: Engage in a shared craft. Whether it's pottery, painting, or DIY, it's about the shared moments, not perfection.
- **Old-school Gaming**: Revisit classic board games or video games. A sprinkle of friendly rivalry and a dash of nostalgia can be a great combo.
- **Routine Breakers**: A short getaway can reignite connections. A slight change can do wonders, whether it's a serene cabin or a beachfront view.

- **Notes of Affection**: Pen down your emotions. Surprise notes or random messages can express sentiments that often remain unspoken in daily routines.

In the whirlwind called parenting, taking out moments exclusively for each other is like choosing the scenic route. And it's worth every deviation.

SECTION 3: NAVIGATING SOCIAL EXPECTATIONS AND STEREOTYPES

Fatherhood has often been misunderstood, thanks to age-old stereotypes. These range from the comical (inept dads, overwhelmed by diapers) to the clichéd (dads whose culinary expertise stops at ordering pizza). Let's set the record straight.

Each time you engage in hands-on parenting, be it comforting your child late at night, sneaking veggies into their meals, or showcasing those 'rear-view' eyes parents supposedly have, you're reshaping perceptions. We, as contemporary dads, are not mere spectators. We're equal stakeholders, traversing the unpredictable world of parenting with commitment and genuine emotion.

The essence of modern fatherhood transcends superhero capes. It's about being present, adapting, and being everything, our child needs. The real superpower lies in debunking myths, showcasing that today's dads are a blend of love, laughter, and, yes, an endless supply of classic dad jokes.

Dealing With Societal Stereotypes About Dad Duties

Gone should be the days when fathers are painted as couch potatoes, BBQ aficionados, emotionless beings, or those lost when faced with a diaper. Let's redefine this portrayal.

- **Shared Duties**: Whether it's changing diapers or narrating bedtime stories, we're in sync with our partners.
- **Embracing Emotions**: Feelings aren't gender-specific. Children should see their fathers express a wide range of emotions. It's a part of being human.
- **Work-life Synergy**: Juggling work and family can be an acrobatic feat, but it's a balance we aim for.
- **Active Nurturers**: We're more than babysitters. We're the lead actors in this parenting storyline, from pretend tea parties to serious homework sessions.
- **Breaking Gender Norms**: We're multifaceted. We can flip pancakes, fix things around the house, and be present for our kids, proving labels are restrictive and unnecessary.
- **Allies in Partnership**: We're active contributors in the partnership, facing challenges and cherishing dreams together.
- **Challenging the "Tough Guy" Image**: Our interests are diverse, from action films to baking shows, from supporting at dance recitals to comforting a child after a minor mishap.

Here's to the contemporary fathers, redefining norms, dismantling outdated beliefs, and setting a new gold standard. It's time to embrace our roles and maybe change a diaper or two in style.

Overcoming Feelings of Inadequacy or Uncertainty in Your Parenting Skills

Take a moment, breathe, and recognize this undeniable fact: You are in the company of every parent who ever lived. Feeling lost? Join the club. Parenting doesn't come with an owner's manual, but it does provide a unique field of trial and error. Think less about assembling flat-packed furniture and more about sculpting a masterpiece over time. You'll stumble, you'll fumble, but most importantly, you'll learn.

Those baffled stares from your little ones? It's not just you. They're often as puzzled as we are. It's a shared journey, a guessing game, and it's one of the most rewarding ones you'll ever play.

Confidence is key. Consider yourself a master artist in the world of parenting. Yes, there will be mess, but there's beauty in chaos. You have a natural intuition for this. Trust it.

Here's a roadmap for those moments when doubt creeps in:

- **Embrace the Journey**: Parenting is a constant learning curve. Perfection isn't the goal. Growth is.
- **Trust Yourself**: You know your child. Trust your instincts; they're there for a reason.
- **Connect with Others**: Talk to other parents. Shared experiences can offer both comfort and wisdom.

- **Avoid Comparisons**: Every parent's journey is unique. Celebrate the victories, no matter how small.
- **Laugh Often**: Even in the chaos, find joy. A good laugh can lighten any load.
- **Quality Time Matters**: This is where bonds are forged, and confidence grows.
- **Seek Help if Needed**: Whether it's a partner or a professional, don't hesitate to reach out.
- **Be Kind to Yourself**: Give yourself credit. Parenting is tough; it's okay to take a breath.
- **Acknowledge Success**: Every smile and every laugh from your child is a win.
- **Be Present**: Ultimately, it's not about having all the answers. It's about being there.

We're all in this together, navigating the unknown, doing our best, and learning as we go. Doubts? Sure, we all have them. But if you find yourself in need of a lift, remember that a well-timed smile or a shared laugh with your child is sometimes all the reassurance you need. Because in this whirlwind tour of parenting, the heart and the humor are what genuinely guide us.

Building Confidence in Your Unique Style of Fatherhood

Confidence as a dad isn't about following a script; it's about discovering your role. It's uncharted territory, and you are the adventurous explorer. Your unique style, intuition, and love for your child will guide your way. Here's a little nudge to help you along:

- **Own Your Uniqueness**: You're not just any dad. You're their dad. Your individuality isn't a quirk; it's a feature.
- **Trust Yourself**: Fatherhood comes with built-in instincts. Your gut feelings aren't just random; they're your subconscious wisdom talking.
- **Learn but Adapt**: Advice from other dads is valuable, but it's a buffet, not a set menu. Take what suits you and your little one.
- **Celebrate Everything**: The small wins are still wins. Your child's smile? That's a standing ovation.
- **Be There, Truly There**: Presence isn't about proximity. It's about connection. That's where confidence grows.
- **Learn as You Go**: Every stumble in parenting is a step forward. Embrace the mess, the mystery, and the magic of growth.
- **Laugh it Off**: Perfection is a myth. Your child won't remember the flawless days, but they'll cherish the fun, imperfect ones.
- **Lean on Your Team**: Share the highs and lows with those around you. They're not just your support network; they're your cheering squad.
- **Quality Over Quantity**: Time with your child isn't about the clock; it's about the connection. Make it count.
- **Reflect and Revel**: Take stock of your journey. You're not just raising a child; you're evolving as a human.

There's no universal dad manual because there's no universal dad. Your unique style isn't just acceptable; it's essential. Your quirks, your humor, your love—they're the very things that make you the incredible dad you are. Embrace the adventure. Enjoy the ride. And remember, in this thrilling world of parenting, your love and your presence are the North Star guiding your way.

SECTION 4: FATHERHOOD AND MENTAL HEALTH

Section 4 is all about an essential topic that often goes unspoken—fatherhood and mental health. It's crucial to acknowledge that being a dad comes with its share of joys and challenges, and it's okay to prioritize your mental well-being throughout this journey.

Understanding the Signs of Paternal Postnatal Depression (PPND)

Just like moms, dads can also experience postnatal depression, and it's essential to understand the signs to take care of our mental health.

Becoming a father is a monumental shift in a man's life, filled with incredible joy but also real challenges. Among those challenges, Paternal Postnatal Depression (PPND) is one that often goes unspoken, yet it's vital to recognize. It's not just about feeling a bit down; it's an actual condition that requires understanding and compassion. Here's what you need to know:

- **Mood Changes**: It's natural to feel a range of emotions, but constant sadness or irritability shouldn't be ignored. If mood swings become extreme, take note.

- **Chronic Fatigue**: Sure, parenting is tiring, but persistent fatigue, even with rest, could signal something more.
- **Loss of Interest**: Pulling away from friends, family, or hobbies you love? It could be a sign of PPND.
- **Appetite Shifts**: Drastic changes in eating habits aren't just about stress. They might be a signal for you to pause and reflect.
- **Physical Symptoms**: Unexplained headaches, stomach problems, or body aches without any apparent cause can be linked to PPND. Those unexplained aches and pains might not just be random. Listen to your body; it might be telling you something.
- **Bonding Struggles**: Difficulty connecting with your baby isn't a failure; it could be a symptom. It doesn't make you any less of a loving dad.
- **Feeling Worthless**: Negative self-talk is more than just being hard on yourself. Remember, you are vital to your family.
- **Anger and Agitation**: More irritable than usual? It might be time to seek understanding, not judgment.
- **Concentration Issues**: Challenges in focusing or decision-making might be more than fatigue. It might be a sign to seek help.
- **Thoughts of Harm**: This is serious. If thoughts of self-harm or harm to others occur, seek professional assistance immediately.

It's essential to recognize that experiencing one or more of these signs doesn't necessarily mean you have PPND. However, awareness is crucial. Mental health isn't a side note; it's central to being the best dad you can be.

What to Do

- **Talk About It**: Open up to your partner, friends, or family. It's not a weakness; it's a strength.
- **Seek Professional Help if Needed**: Counselors, therapists, and healthcare providers are there for a reason.
- **Take Care of Yourself**: Exercise, eat well, and take moments for yourself. Self-care isn't selfish; it's foundational.

In this journey of fatherhood, recognizing the signs of PPND is vital. It's not about "manning up;" it's about being human and understanding that it's okay to seek help. You're not in this alone, and seeking support isn't a failure; it's part of the journey towards becoming an even more incredible dad.

The Importance of Self-Care for Dads

My buddy Sam has a saying – *"In the Fatherhood Marathon, Don't Forget Your Pit Stops."*

Look, dad-life is no walk in the park. It's more like a never-ending obstacle course where we're trying to be the best versions of ourselves for the family MVPs we care about most. But here's the kicker: to genuinely be there for them, we've got to be there for ourselves, too. It's not about navel-gazing; it's about being present, charged up, and ready to tackle the dad role with all its ups, downs, and in-betweens.

- **Be Your Best Version**: Imagine running on a full tank. You're sharper, chirpier, and, let's face it, a lot less likely to misplace the car keys. That's the version your family loves to see.
- **Mental Gymnastics**: From decoding baby cries to navigating preteen angst, the dad brain gets quite the workout. Some good ol' self-care can keep that burnout at bay.
- **The Emotion Spectrum**: From those heart-melting first steps to the tantrum at aisle three, emotions can be a rollercoaster. Regular self-check-ins can keep us grounded.
- **Lead by Example**: Ever notice those mini-me versions trying to emulate every move we make? Let's show them how to value themselves by taking care of numero uno (that's you).

Dad-Care: How-To Guide:

- **Old Passions, New Dad**: Those guitar lessons, Sunday morning golf rounds, or vintage comic collections? They're not just nostalgia; they're your sanctuary.
- **Move It, Don't Lose It**: Doesn't have to be a triathlon. Could be a brisk walk, maybe backyard soccer, or just chasing the little ones around. Stay active; stay fresh.
- **Sleep: The Unsung Hero**: Grabbing those Z's is crucial. Recharge, refuel, and, if possible, avoid late-night infomercial rabbit holes.

- **Speak Up, Reach Out**: Talking things out can be therapeutic. Whether it's friends, family, or pros, every now and then unloading is the best reload.
- **Golden 'Me' Moments**: Find that quiet corner, that perfect playlist, or that book gathering dust. A little you-time can go a long way.

Being a top-notch dad isn't about perfection. It's about intention, love, and understanding that taking care of yourself isn't a side quest - it's part of the main mission. Take that pit stop, recharge, and keep running that incredible race. As fathers, we often prioritize the well-being of our families over our own, but taking care of ourselves is just as vital. Self-care is not selfish; it's essential for our mental, emotional, and physical health.

TILL NEXT TIME

Gather 'round, Team Dad, think of yourself as a Swiss army knife: versatile, ready for anything, and occasionally used to open bottles. Armed with wit, dad jokes, and a newfound know-how, you're set to conquer the wild terrain of fatherhood. Dive into those murky waters, relish the peaks, and don't forget to take a breather in those picture-perfect moments.

Now, if this guide felt like a trusty sidekick on your heroic dad journey, please toss a quick review on Amazon. It's less about boosting my ego and more about guiding the next band of dad warriors to this trusty roadmap. As a thank you, go to ultimatedads.com for some awesome bonus content.

Here's the real deal - you're equipped, resilient, and one fantastic dad. Fatherhood's landscape keeps shifting, but you're the adaptable hero in this tale. Keep evolving, keep loving, and keep being the rock star dad you are. Onward to more diaper changes and bedtime stories, champions!

REFERENCES

Bellefonds, C. de. (2022, December 28). 17 Ways to relieve morning sickness. What to Expect. https://www.whattoexpect.com/pregnancy/morning-sickness/

Ben-Joseph, E. P. (2018). Birth plans (for parents). KidsHealth. https://kidshealth.org/en/parents/birth-plans.html

Casell, A. (2021). A childbirth cheat sheet for dads-to-be. BabyCenter. https://www.babycenter.com/pregnancy/relationships/a-childbirth-cheat-sheet-for-dads-to-be_8244

Cleveland Clinic. (2019, September 16). Yes, postpartum depression in men is very real. https://health.clevelandclinic.org/yes-postpartum-depression-in-men-is-very-real/

Cleveland Clinic. (2022, April 12). Postpartum depression: Types, symptoms, treatment & prevention. https://my.clevelandclinic.org/health/diseases/9312-postpartum-depression

Dellecese, M. M. (2015, January 23). The benefits of reading to baby in womb. Green Child Magazine. https://www.greenchildmagazine.com/reading-to-baby-in-womb/

Dewar, G. (2017, January 2). Newborn sleep patterns: A survival guide. Parenting Science. https://parentingscience.com/newborn-sleep/

dopedadcollective. (2023, May 22). Decoding baby's sleep signals: 10 signs your baby is sleepy. https://dopedadco.com/baby-sleep-signals/

Health Partners. (2021, May 6). 13 tips for father-baby bonding. HealthPartners Blog. https://www.healthpartners.com/blog/tips-for-father-baby-bonding/

India, C. (2018, May 21). Dad diary: Baby starts kicking. Cordlife India. https://www.cordlifeindia.com/blog/dad-diary-baby-starts-kicking/

John, S. (2020, June 10). The 15 best quotes about fatherhood you will ever hear. The Manual. https://www.themanual.com/culture/best-fatherhood-quotes/

Kelly, K. (2022). Labor & delivery support tips just for dads. Parents. https://www.parents.com/pregnancy/giving-birth/labor-support/labor-delivery-advice-dads/

Khurana, S. (2019). Who said the "Child is father of the man"? ThoughtCo. https://www.thoughtco.com/child-is-the-father-of-man-3975052

LaBracio, J. (2023). Everything you need to pack in your hospital bag. Babylist. https://www.babylist.com/hello-baby/what-to-pack-in-your-hospital-bag

Mead Johnson. (n.d.). Hospital bag checklist for baby and mom. Enfamil Canada. Retrieved July 13, 2023, from https://www.enfamil.ca/blogs/pregnancy-development-calendar-month-9/what-to-pack-for-delivery-hospital-bag-checklist-for-baby-and-mom

Mihalich-Levin, L. (2022, August 13). How to advocate for family-friendly benefits at your workplace. Mindful Return. https://www.mindfulreturn.com/advocate/

Moon, R. (2019). How to keep your sleeping baby safe: AAP policy explained. HealthyChildren.org. https://www.healthychildren.org/English/ages-stages/baby/sleep/Pages/A-Parents-Guide-to-Safe-Sleep.aspx

Pampers. (2021). Baby proofing your house. https://www.pampers.co.uk/baby/baby-proofing/article/baby-proofing-your-home

Pampers. (2022). Couvade syndrome: All about men's pregnancy symptoms. https://www.pampers.com/en-us/pregnancy/pregnancy-symptoms/article/couvade-syndrome

Pitman, T. (2009, August 4). Understand your baby's cries. Today's Parent. https://www.todaysparent.com/baby/baby-development/understand-your-babys-cries/

Sweeney, K. (2020). How to heal your baby's diaper rash. Children's Hospital Los Angeles. https://www.chla.org/blog/advice-experts/how-heal-your-babys-diaper-rash

Taylor, B. (2018, May 22). What to do when your birth plan takes an unexpected twist. Direct Advice for Dads. https://directadvicefordads.com.au/expecting/what-to-do-when-your-birth-plan-takes-an-unexpected-twist/

The Brussels Times. (n.d.). Father's touch equally important for baby's development as mother's, research shows. https://www.brusselstimes.com/88207/fathers-touch-as-important-for-babys-development-as-mothers-research-shows-vub-skin-caress-stress-resistant-free-university-of-brussels-liverpool-frontiers-of-physiology

Unicef. (n.d.). How music affects your baby's brain: Mini parenting master class. Retrieved July 11, 2023, from https://www.unicef.org/parenting/child-development/how-music-affects-your-babys-brain-class

University of South Australia. (n.d.). Why is newborn baby skin-to-skin contact with dads and non-birthing parents important? Here's what the science says. https://www.unisa.edu.au/unisanews/2022/september/story3/

VanAlstyne, L. (2019, April 14). Tips for dads in the delivery room (Like how to not pass out). Mother Rising. https://www.motherrisingbirth.com/2019/04/tips-for-dads-in-the-delivery-room.html

Walsh, G. (2019, October 16). Skin-to-skin contact between father and baby is vitally important. The Irish Times. https://www.irishtimes.com/life-and-style/health-family/skin-to-skin-contact-between-father-and-baby-is-vitally-important-1.4042648

Weiss, K. (2021). How to talk to your baby. What to Expect. https://www.whattoexpect.com/first-year/milestones/how-to-talk-to-babies

Williamson, A. (2022). Five ways to survive relationship changes after having a baby. Hitched. https://www.hitched.co.uk/wedding-planning/organising-and-planning/relationship-changes-after-having-a-baby/

Yang, N., Shi, J., Lu, J., & Huang, Y. (2021). Language development in early childhood: Quality of teacher-child interaction and children's receptive vocabulary competency. Frontiers in Psychology, 12. https://doi.org/10.3389/fpsyg.2021.649680

Made in the USA
Middletown, DE
22 March 2024

51910240R00086